Wholesome Parenting:
Paving a Brighter and Kinder Future with Our Children

Lindsay Swanberg

Published by Dragonfly Moon Press

ISBN: 9781072715634

**It is easier to build strong
children than to repair broken
men.**
-Frederick Douglass (1818-1895)

TABLE OF CONTENTS

INTRODUCTION

As of 2019, I've been working closely with children for 17 years, and raising my own family of children for 21. In 2002, when my eldest was four and my second child was on the way, and to be able to afford to stay home with my kids, I started my own full-time, home-based child care program. I quickly learned that supporting children is one of my most natural talents and biggest passions in life. In that time, I have taken hundreds of hours of training in child development, early childhood education and curriculum, and finally completed my degree with an extra, year-long focus on teaching infants through preschool age. I've worked happily and successfully with dozens of children and their families, in this time, and I eventually joyfully went on to expand my business into a certified preschool child care program, with a larger group of children and assistant teacher employees.

Growing as a parent and teacher, then, has been the main focus of my entire adult life. I'm immensely thankful for the way this time and experience has enriched my heart and life and very being! It's my deepest pleasure to share what I have learned with other parents who are still paving their way, in this very personal territory. All families are different in their own ways, after all. We *all* have our own strengths and weaknesses, as human beings, when it comes to doing our best with our families. My intent here is to help supplement parental instincts and skills with my experience and insights that haven't yet been seen by those who are currently less experienced with children. Really, we can all always learn something from someone else. Learning and growing as parents may take patience and humility, but the outcome is worth the effort in that it makes us so much stronger! It makes our families stronger, our parenting more conscious and conscientious, our relationships closer, *and* our children benefit greatly in seeing us give the whole family all we've got. It gives our children their best possible future, and their best childhood memories of us. What a gift!

This is, in fact, such an important process for our families, that I've been writing about children for years. It began as me blogging in my spare time, my thoughts and feelings on those lessons and insights which I have found most valuable. Now that I'm expanding on my written pieces in book form, I am including some of my blog material here. It's too meaningful not to.

Everyone benefits from us knowing how to relate to the children of this world better. And how to communicate, respect, reason with, and support them more authentically. Humanity is strengthened by our leaps into emotional intelligence, by those of us willing to pave the way. Thank you for bringing your heart to the table, when it comes to doing right by children.

CHAPTER 1

Wholesome Parenting

Wholesome parenting contains the philosophy that knowing more about healthy parenting means we can provide more as parents to our children and families; it intends to offer a more complete view of raising grounded, nourished, and happy kids. *Wholesome* parenting means approaching our parenting practice from a more well-rounded understanding of what children need from us to support them in becoming their healthiest and happiest selves. It means we intentionally put as much of our hearts into this process as possible, while working to leave our ego, fears, and past traumas outside the door of our relationships with our children. It means being willing to look at our parenting from as many angles as possible. It means bringing our whole self to the table. Wholesome parenting is trustworthy, safe, patient, kind, consistent, playful, joyful, and *connected*. I'll explain how.

First, let me ask you what your favorite childhood memories are. Who gave you a sense of security and reliability? Who believed in you, the way you needed most? Now, who scared, embarrassed, or hurt you? Do you remember how much that brought you down, and probably for no reason? Imagine a world in which the latter rarely happens because people have evolved to be better to themselves and to each other. We can break the chains of pain that often get handed down. We can bring to children the best we've ever known, and more. It begins with awareness, and is fueled by bravery.

It can take emotional bravery to set down our pride, to ask a child for forgiveness, to show them adults can be wrong, too, or to treat a child as an equal when we were not shown the same respect in our own childhood. This process isn't meant to be belittling to adults in any way -that's detrimental to children, too. It's detrimental for children to feel powerful *over* adults, and to learn they can hurt adults instead of being the ones hurt by adults. It can take humility and receptivity to be able to teach a child to laugh *with* each other instead of at each other. The key is mutual respect and a relationship built on integrity. This type of parenting, then, is meant to be humbling and opening so we may connect to each other in new and stronger ways: love and integrity-based ways, for the truest and deepest connections.

For the truth is that human beings are sustained by a sense of connection. We are social mammals, by nature, who long to be needed and appreciated by our "tribe." This instinct is a core-deep urge for survival: part of us knows we won't get far alone. We see an example of this in the experiment done decades ago, by Harry Harlow, proving that hungry baby monkeys would rather be held by a mother-like monkey than just fed her milk. Monkeys growing up without mothers, in a laboratory, were found by researchers to become so distraught by their loneliness that some of them began starving themselves to death. So, when given the choice between a cold, metal, surrogate "mother" machine that provided them milk, or a soft and textured surrogate "mother" without any milk to offer, the monkeys snuggled the soft and comforting mother instead of the milk-giving mother. The study also showed that the monkeys with a soft and cozy surrogate were emotionally strengthened by her presence, while monkeys without a more realistic surrogate were quite afraid, and constantly attempted measures of self-soothing for their anxiety. We crave and *need* love, support, and a sense of place and family, in our world.

In my experience, all children particularly need and thrive on having parents who are emotionally stable, open, forgiving, affectionate, and attentive. Children gain *so much* from those of us who are willing to engage with them on their level: playing, laughing, enjoying the moment, exploring the world with open-minded curiosity and open communication, forgiving and moving on, and longing to learn as much as possible about the world through their senses: touch, art, music, smell, taste, hearing, sight, and emotional feelings. Often, most of us have lost a lot of these qualities. "Growing up" has taken them away from us, or matured them in us. We trade our interest in play and joy and being open, for protecting ourselves in a harsh and fast-paced society, and for getting the bills paid.

Relating to children in a better way, then, is also nourishing for *us*. It feeds a part of us we never should've had to part from in the first place -which can be painful at first, until we face it, embrace it, and fully move into it. It reawakens a side of us that is more open, more joyous, more ready to connect.

11

Remember, for a moment, what it felt like to play games with your friends as a young child, to lie in the tall grass within an aura of quiet sunshine, to freely swing with the breeze blowing through your hair. Or to be snuggled in the arms of a loving parent or family member. Or how exciting lunch time was after playing hard outside all morning. How good it felt to submerge yourself into a warm bath, with only your toys and their lives that you created, and not a care about the rest of the world outside. We were connected to the moment and to enjoying our lives. So many of us spend our adult lives trying to get that back, or wondering what's missing. The more we give to our children, on their level, the more we heal the void within us.

Adults, it turns out, in giving up the joys and freedoms of childhood, have often turned to subconsciously adopting coping mechanisms for the requirements, burdens, and responsibilities of adulthood. For example, spinning and jumping and swinging and playing may have become having drinks at the bar after work. Writing, drawing, singing, and creating works of heart may have become watching TV that helps us laugh or unwind, at the end of the day, while consuming easy, tasty junk food on the couch. Diving into the internet may have replaced the quiet solitude of enjoying the moment, or the vulnerability of having a long conversation with a good friend. We hide our lives in these things, unsure of how to connect with life like we used to. But we only have these lives of ours for so long. Why not tap into the things that used to speak to us and bring us joy, while we still have time?

We do this with children when we recognize that:

- Every time they speak to us, they are looking for *connection with us* more than looking for attention for their topic of discussion. If they point out a bird in the sky, a bug on the ground, a shadow in their room, a need to go potty, a hungry tummy, a love of *anything,* they are asking us to join their world for a moment. They may also have a need to be met (hunger or pottying, etc.), but they are also demonstrating a longing to feel connected to us, and this is how they attempt connection with their guardians.

- We show them that we value *them* when we show attention, curiosity, and support to their interests, fears, values, feelings, and questions.

- Being present in the moment with a child shows them we value the world bubble within which they live. We want to be a part of it. We're willing to enter that zone with them. We like it there. And it conveys that adults can be present in the moment, too, instead of distracted by thoughts of the past or future. We show them that we don't *have* to completely give this quality of presence and awareness up as we grow.

- Play and joy and connection are the remedies to a world that can be unexplainable, alienating, violent, lonely, confusing, degrading, and abrasive. We can build a foundation of the former that weathers the storms of the latter. We can build hearts that thrive on bringing play and joy and connection into the world to heal it, in the face of the world's sufferings.

- We demonstrate how to stay connected to ourselves, our loved ones, and our own precious lives by living joyously, by enjoying our hobbies passionately, by making time to enjoy the hobbies of those whom we love, by exploring and building up our own interests and areas of joy. For me, my adult play (AKA joyous hobbies) includes writing, meditating, the chanting of my Nichiren Buddhist practice, nature walks, live music, jigsaw puzzles, travel and day trips, homemade food, delicious restaurant food, outings with friends, swimming and bubble baths. Growing up, my children saw me make time for these things, and include them where appropriate. To support their joyous play and hobbies, I spent hours building Lego structures with them,

14

taking them to the park, going on long family walks and bike rides to the movie theater, making fun games out of drawing "competitions," and more.

• The family that plays together, laughs together, and trusts and relies on each other, is typically the healthiest, happiest, and most fulfilled family.

Play, joy, connection, and trust are the antidotes to the harsher side of life. They are what fulfill us, what we all thrive on, and what heal us. The opposite of these things, for children, are parental anger, sarcasm, and emotional instability. To be blunt, these characteristics poison the well-being of our young ones. These kinds of outbursts teach children that they are not safe at home, which breaks trust, and amplifies insecurity. When children feel consistently insecure, they seek ways in their lives to feel powerful again. This may be externalized through defiance, temper tantrums, lying, manipulating, etc. Or it may be internalized as becoming a people-pleaser (attempting to find a sense of value through approval from others -which takes away our own sense of self and instincts for healthy boundaries), or a caregiver to their adults -a role reversal that children should *not* know the burden of bearing. Or it may be internalized as seeking attention through feeling victimized, depressed, or helpless. Clearly, while children need us to enter their world and help sustain it by relating to them and enjoying who they are on their level through means of play, joy, and connection, they also need us to provide them with a home environment and family lifestyle of emotional stability and support.

Additionally, sarcasm and anger impair the nature of the child's inner voice -that voice they are developing as they grow up that plays in the background of their minds for the rest of their lives, telling them what to do, who they are, who to trust, what decisions and judgment calls to go forward with, what they deserve and are worth, and how to live. If we are sarcastic and unforgiving with them, they eventually will be too. If we are too critical with them, they eventually will be too. If we take out our anger issues on them, they will learn to live with that cloud of darkness and anger, within themselves, as if it were normal, too.

Depression in parents is also linked to lower levels of emotional warmth, lowered quality of interactions, and a generally weakened supporting of the children. The physical, emotional, and cognitive well-being of children can go undernourished by parents who feel crushed by depression. It's hard to give enough to our kids when we are under the weight of feeling like we aren't enough. I know this reality intimately; I've been there, and I was raised by parents who lived there as well. I call on you with all of my heart to do your best to put that aside for your children, though. Even if you do it in baby steps. I beseech you to give all you can while you are still here with the opportunity to give it. Sometimes doing this for others is exactly what saves us from ourselves.

We all have our own work to do: we all have pain from our pasts to heal, and to keep separate from the relationships we create with our babies; we all have pain that haunts us, and our daily sources of stress. So, we must set out to gain awareness, stay more centered, and work on our emotional weak spots. We owe that much to ourselves and to our children. Having an understanding of how we facilitate our individual parenting styles, in the meantime, can make a huge improvement in our family relationships and dynamics! There are several different main parenting styles, and it's important to understand the effect they will have on your children and family.

Authoritarian parenting: This old-fashioned style of parenting is hindering to children and families, and sometimes detrimental to a child's development, in that authoritarian parenting demands that the child obey the parents at all times, whether or not they understand why; it's low on attentiveness and interaction with the child, it's low in communicating and in both showing and supporting feelings, and children are expected to be seen and not heard unless spoken to. The child's expression is not welcome, or is only welcome to a certain, very limited extent. The child's uniqueness, questions, interests, feelings, and feedback for parents is quite limited in how much the parents welcome it. The parents expect the child to keep themselves to themselves, expect the least amount of parenting from the parents, and obediently do as they are told at all times. This method is parent-centered and punishment oriented. It can feel to the kids like being jailed in their own home and family.

Authoritative parenting: The healthiest form of parenting, and family-centered, it provides a well-rounded balance between caring warmly for the child's thoughts, feelings, expression, and input, and providing thoughtful, considerate, *consistent*, high quality guidance and discipline for the child's behavior. The children thrive on this method thanks to the attentiveness and healthy structure these parents provide. The children are heard, included, respected, and encouraged; they are given a healthy set of boundaries and standards to live by, wherein they know where they end and the parent begins, they know exactly what the parents expect from them and how to reach those healthy goals and expectations, they know they will be supported by their parents when they stumble in their endeavors, and they have developed a strong voice within the family by growing up in such a supportive and encouraging family; these children develop a strong, positive sense of self.

Permissive parenting: This method, in which the child tends to call the shots with the parent (or tantrum for their way until they get it, for example), and have an unstructured lifestyle due to the parent's inability to create routine and expectations that are stuck to, is child-centered. Revolving around the child, it is too lenient. The parent acquiesces to the whims and demands of the child, doesn't provide enough structure, consistency, and boundary-setting, and teaches the child that s/he doesn't have to earn the things s/he wants. It gives the child too much power and free reign in the family. When a child feels in charge without better guidance from her parents, it's confusing, unsettling, and creates power struggles. Children of this parenting style often become overbearing to overcome the sense of insecurity they feel by having so much power over their guardians. It can feel to the kids like dangling from a thread at a great and dangerous height with no one to help you up.

Neglectful/Uninvolved parenting: Here, the parent has taken permissive parenting to the next level. This method of parenting is cold, aloof, disinterested, distant or absent, self-absorbed, and/or rejecting. The child is left on their own without much guidance, supervision, discipline, input, or care from the parent. This style is detrimental to the well-being of young people, and I would argue that it's blatantly abusive. It can feel to the kids like they are worthless and unlovable human beings.

Children have different temperaments, and understanding them helps us support our child the way *they* need supporting. According to *Infants, Toddlers, and Caregivers: A Curriculum of Respectful, Responsive, Relationship-Based Care and Education:*

> "Temperament is an individual's behavioral style and unique way of responding to the world. It involves a set of personality characteristics that are influenced by nature (genetics) and by nurture (interactions). These unique patterns of emotional and motor reactions begin with numerous genetic instructions that guide brain development and then are affected by the prenatal and postnatal environment. As an individual infant continues to develop, the specific experiences she has and the social context of her life

19

influence the nature and expression of her temperament (p.216)."

The temperament of a child is classified as slow-to-warm, easy going, or feisty. So, let's take a look at what these mean.

Slow-to-warm children are more shy or reserved with new people, might become afraid and sad easily, are less interested in new experiences rather than the things they already know and love, and often seek adult guidance, support, and protection from trusted caregivers. These young ones need a safety zone, patience in assisting them with social adaptation, and to experience positive interactions regularly. They are typically very sensitive and need a lot of bubble space. They need consistent routines that everyone follows and respects, and they need their personal boundaries and physical bodies respected by everyone around them. They need parents who consistently display to them that they are safe in their bodies. They respond best to gentleness, patience, respect, and consistency.

Easy going children get along with others easily, are happy, calm, and friendly in their demeanor, typically having positive and stable emotions and interactions with others, are reliable, and are comfortable letting feisty children take over (something to watch out for; these children might need help asserting their boundaries). These young ones adjust to new experiences and people pretty easily. They are interested in the world, are easy to care for, and respond best to the qualities of easy-going behavior: kindness, warmth, positivity, patience, stable emotions, and clear reason.

Feisty children want to lead and feel in charge, can be quick to anger, or easily irritated in general, can overpower other people's boundaries in an attempt to feel their own needs are being met (grabbing a toy from another child, screaming for food, hitting for a blanket, fighting often), and are otherwise intense and unpredictable in nature. They are often loud and/or domineering of the situation and environment. It's important for these children to learn where they end and everyone else begins, and to have healthy outlets for their energy and urges. These young ones need a lot of physical activity, concrete language when we communicate with them, clear choices without much wiggle room, the fortifying of *others'* boundaries, constant support in respecting other people's boundaries, and a heavy focus on supporting the development of empathy for others. Giving them developmentally-appropriate leadership tasks can be helpful in directing them. They respond best to a "power *with* you" instead of "power *over* you" approach from adults; feisty children have a strong sense of feeling powerful that they want respected. It's our job to find the balance between that and teaching them to also respect others, instead of potentially steamrolling their peers and caregivers.

Wholesome parenting is also peaceful parenting. We implement peaceful parenting by treating our children kindly and respectfully, by setting the important example of loving *ourselves* kindly and

21

respectfully, by creating a forgiving, compassionate, empathetic, attentive, affectionate, joyful, safe, and gentle home environment and family dynamic, and by communicating with each other openly and peacefully. The act of communicating peacefully may sound like merely avoiding curse words and name-calling, but it's so much more than that.

In the first few years of life, children need us to (respectfully) mirror them with our speech; they need us to acknowledge, verbally, what they are doing -and what we're doing, when we catch them observing us. This may sound like, "Oh! You found your other shoe! Good, let's get that on so we can go to the park. I'm putting your shoe on your left foot. Now we're ready to go!" Or it may be more intimate, "I can tell you're so sad right now (*hugs the child*). I'm sorry you feel sad. Can I help? What can I do?" Or it may be something like responding to them pointing to a cup with, "That's your cup. Would you like it?" This teaches them language skills, shows them we are paying attention to their needs, and shows them the line of communication between us is open.

Taken a little further, it's highly valuable to be able to recognize when an emotional situation is "their problem" or "my problem," and then incorporate that into our communication with each other. It helps determine the best approach for responding to the thing that is upsetting one of us. For example, if a child is having big feelings about their friend grabbing a toy away from them, is this current situation about their needs, or about mine? It's about their needs when they need support for *their* feelings; it's about my needs when I have a need for support of *my* feelings. I'll explain this further to clarify.

If they're upset that their friend took their toy, what I have to do is very simple: I must show them I understand their feelings, and that I'm willing to try to help. Really, when we get this technique down, it's immensely valuable to our relationships. Most people, at the heart of things, want to know that they are understood and that their loved one wants to support them and their needs. So, going forward, let's always aim to keep our responses to them this simple.

That looks like this:

1. **Mirror how they feel back to them:** "I see you're angry that your friend took your toy. That would make me feel bad, too!"

2. **How can I help?** "Can I help you talk to your friend about not grabbing your toys?"

Another example, let's say they're melting down over hunger:

1. **Mirror:** "Oh my goodness, your tummy must be so hungry!"

2. **Help:** "Let's get you some food!" ...or... "Lunch will be ready in 20

minutes. Do you want a glass of milk while you wait?"

This being about supporting *their* feelings (instead of my own), there would be no need for me to add my expectations, desires, disappointments, or biases into the conversation. There would be *no use* for a lecture. Like, I wouldn't need to say, "Now, go be a nice friend," or "stop being a baby!" Peaceful communication, in our parenting, is meant to take blame, shame, name-calling, embarrassment, and rejection/disconnection out of the process. We should stick to the method of reflecting their feelings back to them to show we understand how they feel and why, and offer to help. *That* is genuine, peaceful support. *Later* we can return to talking about what happened if we need to teach the child a new boundary, or discuss our own feelings.

If *I* become upset because my angry child grabbed the toy back from the other child and hurt them in the process, however, it becomes a "me problem," in that I now have a boundary I need to establish (and a problem to solve). This changes the response to my child a bit. I then have to communicate with them:

1. **How I feel:** "It scares me that you hurt your friend to get the toy back. And I feel sad that your friend is hurting now."
2. **Mirror what happened for *them*:** "I know you felt angry when he grabbed

24

it from you, and you wanted to get it back."

3. **What I need in the future:** "Next time, I need you to ask for it back with your words, instead of hurting your friend. If he doesn't listen to you, please come ask me for help. Let's go ask you're hurt friend if he's okay."

Another example, let's say my child intentionally broke my coffee mug:

1. **How I feel:** "Wow, this makes me feel really bad. I love this mug. It's very special to me. It hurts me that you broke it on purpose.

2. **Mirror what happened for *them*:** "You must have been VERY upset to do this. Let's talk about why you decided to break something of mine."

3. **What I need in the future:** "Next time, please come and talk to me about what you need instead of damaging my things and trying to hurt my feelings. Let's go try to fix my mug, now."

Some of these behaviors earn consequences, of course. *Not punishments meant to shame or control your child,* but natural consequences to attempt to repair the damage that was done, and create a learning experience that the child will remember. Do we have our child ask their friend for forgiveness, offer to

25

share the toy, or apologize and try to explain why they got so upset? The answer would depend on what feels right for the child, for it to be sincere (and therein of any value). For my mug, do I have my child help with some extra chores to earn money to buy me a new one? Do we go to the pottery place and spend an afternoon painting each other new coffee mugs? What suits the situation best for the child's greatest learning opportunity?

In summary, a "them problem" is when our child is upset and in need of our support through us showing we understand how they feel, and then offering to do what we can to help. A "me problem" is when something has happened that I dislike, and that causes me to need to communicate a boundary to my child via telling them how I feel about it, that I see what happened for them, and what I need from them in the future.

Let's try some other scenarios to see if you can tell which one is a "me" problem, and which one is a "them" problem. Mark "me" or "them" and then check your answers below. If you haven't become familiar with the differences between them after this, I suggest rereading the above, and journaling to create your own examples, looking at why one is about you, while the other is about the child.

SCENARIO	ME	THEM
1. Your child is sobbing on the floor because they don't want to go		

to Toby's house after school, like planned. They refuse, and protest by throwing a tantrum.		
2. Your child has told you repeatedly that they don't want a bath, but you ran the bath anyway. You've now found them throwing towels and toilet paper into the tub full of water.		
3. Your child comes home from school and refuses to do chores tonight, saying they have too much homework.		
4. Your child comes home from school crying and distraught, saying they have way too much homework to do tonight.		
5. You have a friend and their child over to have a playdate with your own child. You're enjoying a grown-up conversation when you hear screaming from the playroom, and run in to find your son pulling the other child's hair and grabbing their toy.		
6. Your child doesn't like the way another kid is playing on the playground, so they kick her and		

run away.		
7. Your daughter is yelling at you and throwing things in her room, insisting that she's NEVER going to school again!		
8. Your son looks at the vegetables on his dinner plate and declares that he can't eat dinner because his tummy hurts.		

It's crucial to see the difference between these two sets of needs so that we don't mistakenly either try to make our child's situations and feelings all about us, or conversely take out our upset feelings on them. Both of these scenarios take our child, their feelings, their needs, and their potential out of the picture. It's selfish. Can you imagine if your boss treated you this way -either easily triggered whenever you were uncomfortable with something, or blindsiding you with anger when their own feelings got too big? Can you imagine if there were never enough room for *your* thoughts, feelings, and needs? It works wonders to be able to recognize what we're going through so we can then know how to best support each other. What's even more beautiful, is that children model this behavior once they've seen it in action for long enough! Model self-awareness and peaceful communication, and they will someday, too.

Answers:

28

1.) Them - reflect their feelings and ask what you can do to help. Although frustrating for you, this is about their big feelings regarding either Toby's, transitions, leaving you, or something along those lines. They need their feelings to matter and be heard.

2.) ME - your need is that this kind of behavior not happen again. It wasn't appropriate for them to waste resources and make a mess for you out of revenge. They need your help feeling heard, but also seeing the boundary you have around ruining the bath.

3.) ME - your need is that they follow through with their chores, and not have excuses for why they can't. Or maybe you accept them not doing chores tonight, but you feel you need a better system for making sure there's time for both homework and chores, even on homework-heavy nights. This boundary, and new plan, needs to be communicated so your needs (their contribution at home) can be met.

4.) Them - reflect their feelings and ask what you can do to help. They are clearly very upset about being overwhelmed at school. They're not trying to manipulate you out of them doing their chores; they're just emotional and stretched thin. What can you do, as their parent, to help them get their needs met?

5.) ME - your need is that this kind of behavior not happen again, and your child must understand they can't hurt people to take things away from them. The boundary to set is how to get what we want and need from others, while also maintaining their safety and dignity. Your boundary may also be that other parents won't want their children over there, if they're getting hurt. Your child will lose friends, and you could look bad to the community.

6.) ME - your need is that this kind of behavior not happen again, and that your child not hurt or bully others. Your boundary/need would be for your child to communicate without hurting or scaring others.

7.) Them - reflect her feelings and ask what you can do to help. As frustrating as it can be for parents to listen to their children yell and throw things, she will learn on her own that she doesn't want to throw her things, if she breaks something and loses it forever. More important than her things (you can always remove anything you consider too priceless to let her damage), are the big feelings she's having about school. She needs to feel heard

29

and like her parents are there to help her figure out how to get through it. Addressing not yelling and throwing things in the house should come later. Right now, it's about what she needs first.

8.) Them - reflect his feelings and ask what you can do to help. It can be so frustrating for parents whose children refuse to eat anything healthy. Growing up, I always had my children eat their healthy veggies first, before moving on to the tastier food items. When they are hungry enough, they will eat what you give them. Stubbornness eventually subsides when there isn't a power struggle in which to engage. But if his tummy hurts, or he'd rather eat no dinner than a vegetable-ridden dinner, he does deserve some autonomy over his body. Maybe he'll be hungry enough for some healthy fruit in the morning, after a night of no dinner. What can you do to help, if he says his tummy is hurting? Offer to run him a bubble bath, offer to let him try his veggies again later, or let him go lie down in his bed with a book (or homework)?

It's beneficial, as well, when we can remove lectures from our conversations with our children. Children absorb what we model for them, the quality conversations we have together, the moments spent doing something enjoyable, the moments we spend doing things they're interested in, our demeanors, and our actions. They don't want to hear a bunch of angry reminders and warnings about why and how they did something in a way that was not good enough for us. In fact, they stop listening. The left half of their brain stops paying attention to our words, and they begin to feel like they just have to protect themselves from us instead. Lectures harm relationships instead of strengthening them. Can you imagine having to deal with lectures every time someone who saw themselves as more powerful than you and in control of you wanted you to do something differently? I know I'd start to tune out that disconnected, one-sided, negative kind of speech, too. *Real connection is a two-way street.*

Moreover, when it comes to our expectations of our children, the more we lecture/discuss/negotiate/bark at them, instead of taking action when they don't listen the first time, the more they come to realize that *they don't have to do what we want them to* because we'll just continue to talk at them! They learn their power in this type of situation, pretty quickly. If you find yourself lecturing them (or worse: yelling), repeating yourself, or not being listened to, your kiddos have figured out that they can tune you out and get away with it.

On the other hand, if there are natural consequences *every single time* for your child not following a rule, standard, boundary, or expectation that you have already set with them, and if you seek to create a plan *with* them instead of in power *over* them, they will understand that they need to listen to you and your rules. Even more lovely, is that they'll grow up respecting other people better this way, too! They'll hold themselves more accountable for their actions, put more thought into how they affect the other people around them, and be more conscientious of people's boundaries and needs -those of others *and* their own.

Children who learn to be good listeners and respect boundaries early on in life have it much better later in life (and they develop a more secure attachment style, too, which is a critical component of well-being. We'll talk more about attachment styles later). People who aren't good at listening and respecting boundaries tend to lose friendships, sabotage their jobs, hurt their relationships, etc. These things are natural consequences of being self-absorbed. Natural consequences happen at *all* ages. We do our kids a favor by holding them to a higher standard of behavior when they are young, even if they don't understand that at the time.

Let's not forget to model these things, in our day to day lives, instead of just insisting on them from our babies. Being a good listener means:

- hearing where our people are coming from
- allowing them to express themselves without taking them personally or attempting to make what they share revolve around us instead of them
- seeking to understand the feelings and intentions *behind* their words
- reflecting on their needs and how we can support them, and considering how they may apply to us personally
- contemplating the details of what they've shared with us, and showing empathy or support
- asking questions to better understand
- avoiding interrupting
- avoiding monopolizing the conversation: discussions are a two-way street meant to bridge the gaps between us, and allow BOTH people to feel connected and heard

- being reliable in honoring what has been said to us, and the speaker

Having healthy boundaries means knowing and asserting your own, and respecting those of other people. In action, it looks like:

- standing up for yourself
- expecting to be treated the way you deserve
- clarifying when something makes you uncomfortable
- asking for what you need
- saying no / saying yes
- knowing where you end and another person begins and vice versa
- not being a doormat, and not being a steamroller; finding the healthy middle ground between the two
- accounting for everyone's well-being, whenever possible

Being assertive can be scary, in a world that's lacking healthy boundaries. Some people react to assertive behavior as if it's aggression, or worse. They aren't at all the same thing, though. Having a lack of healthy boundaries is so normalized and so common, that when someone reasonably asserts a boundary and says, "This bothers me, so please don't do this," it can be received as, "Why would you do this to me?! YOU are wrong and I reject you!" People have a right to say please stop, or no thank you, though. We have the right to say I want more, I need help, or I need this to change. We have a right to speak up for ourselves. We also have the need for healthy responses from those to whom we are speaking, rather than poor-boundaried, overreacting ones.

If our children absorb our actions and model our behaviors (and they do, typically to a T), it's up to us to show them how to be assertive in positive, healthy, stable ways. On the scale, we have passive behaviors, assertive behaviors, and aggressive behaviors. **Passive** behavior lets other people walk all over them and take whatever they want. They timidly don't stand up for themselves. At the other extreme, **aggressive** behavior seeks to dominate and/or scare everyone into letting them steamroll them. Maybe they're even violent. They don't take no for an answer, and don't respect the feelings and boundaries of others. A blend of these, we have **passive-aggressive** behavior: indirectly trying to bug or hurt someone in a way that can be hard to hold you accountable for. It's sneaky. It's taking jabs at people in a way that is often hard for people to stand up to. The only healthy middle ground here is assertive behavior. **Assertive** behavior says yes when it means yes, says no when it means no, asks for what it needs, respects the wishes of others to the best of its ability - when it hears others asking for what they need- communicates clearly and honestly, and has everyone's best interests in mind.

Assertive parenting is necessary, then. Our children can't emotionally afford for us to passively let them drive behind the wheel of our lives, reversing our roles with each other; our children can't emotionally afford for us to ignore them, steamroll

34

them, and bully them just to have our own way; our children can't emotionally afford for us to take jabs at them, or try to manipulate them to get what we want. Children *need* for us to take the lead in a kind, honest, firm, consistent way, in our parenting. They need to be able to rely on that assertive parenting, knowing we are emotionally stable and won't slip into any of the other unhealthy behaviors with them. When their world feels safe to them, it becomes possible for them to explore being and expressing who they inherently are.

Gonzalez-Mena, Janet, and Dianne Widmeyer Eyer. Infants, Toddlers, and Caregivers: A

Curriculum of Respectful, Responsive, Relationship-Based Care and Education. New York: McGraw Hill, 2012. P

CHAPTER 2

Supporting Children for Their Best Well-Being

As conscientious parents, we should be continuously evaluating how we're influencing and affecting our children, and what they need from us to thrive in childhood and grow into well-rounded and well-adjusted adults. We'll fail as a race if we don't. Human life can't continue to carry on into the ages if we don't leave our planet with better people than the ones who came before us. Fortunately, our children will pass on what we've given them and taught them.

The more kindness, consistency, patience, and empathy we show and teach our children, the more our humanity changes into a kind, patient, stable, and caring one. With this kind of impact, we can make, what would happen if more people understood that children need a LOT of input in those first few years, and can fail to thrive later as adults without it? What would happen if people were commonly taught that the first few years of brain development are the most important?

Although all the emphasis in our American culture seems to be on acquiring a good degree in college in our twenties, and going on to make as much money as possible, the first few years of life are where our attention should be focused first and foremost. That's not to say a good degree isn't valuable, but how far can a person get with that goal, if they don't have the proper and basic foundation for their best thriving, put in place when the brain is still growing and developing? As parents responsible for the upbringing of our children, we must consider and understand the immense impact we have on them, for better or for worse. This is an education en masse that needs to happen! It needs to become common knowledge that early childhood is *the* critical period for brain development, because the young brain develops so fast, or fails to, in our first few years, according to its environment and its experiences, shaping us all for the rest of our lives.

Like a computer, good functioning of the brain will depend on decent wiring, so that it can process and share information via that wiring. This requires the healthy formation of thousands of neural pathways. A neural pathway is a tract in the brain along which information is relayed; the fewer pathways made in the brain, due to negligence during the first few years, the smaller the amount of information it will be able to process. The development of our brains, when we are infants and toddlers, affects us in all of our developmental areas: physical, cognitive, and socio-emotional. That development of our brain in the first four years of life becomes the foundation from which we grow as people for the rest of our lives. As you can see, healthy neural pathway development is critical to development in general.

Because of the incredibly rapid pace at which the brain develops in early childhood, we can help children achieve their highest level of development by providing them with quality experiences and interactions in a nurturing and supportive environment. According to *Infants, Toddlers, and Caregivers: A Curriculum of Respectful, Responsive, Relationship-Based Care and Education,* connections in the brain form depending on an infant's experiences in life:

> The connections used regularly in everyday life become reinforced, or protected, and become part of the brain's 'circuitry.' The human brain at birth is still very immature, so these early learning experiences can have a dramatic effect over time on an infant's growth and learning. In the early years, young brains produce

almost   twice as many synapses as
they will need… By age two, the
number of synapses a toddler has is
similar   to   that   of   an
adult… Experiences activate neural
pathways, and information in the form
of chemical signals gets stored along
the pathways. Repeated experiences
strengthen specific pathways (p.97).

These neural pathways are the foundation for every
area of development in a person and are an important
part of how intelligent a person will become, how
empathetic, how physically strong and capable, how
hormonal, how artistic, how optimistic vs. pessimistic,
how emotionally stable or not, how resilient, how
anti-social, how successful in life, and so much more.

Conversely, this also means that opportunities
for optimal neural pathway development can be
missed and we can, often unintentionally, impede a
child's brain development. When there is a lack of
quality experiences, and quality relationships that
would strengthen these pathways, areas of the brain
can fail to form well. This impairs a child's social
skills, cognitive growth, emotional well-being, etc.
Stunted growth in these areas can be hard or even
impossible to reverse later in life. "Windows of
opportunity' are sensitive periods in children's lives
when specific types of learning take place… A child's
experiences, good or bad, influence the wiring of his
brain and the connection in his nervous system… If a
child receives little stimulation early on, the synapses
will not develop, and the brain will make fewer

connections" (Graham). Sadly, an impairment of development can also occur from chronic stress and traumas in a child's life.

There's a lot of information circulating on the web, on TV shows, at the doctor's office, and pretty much everywhere we go, about the harmful effects of stress. The body's "fight or flight" response to stress (a production of the hormones cortisol, adrenaline, and norepinephrine) was great when we were cave-moms, always on the go to protect ourselves and our babies from wild beasts that we couldn't turn around and kill and eat. It still serves us well when we need the extra boost to make it through an especially tough challenge or to run from danger. Chronic stress, however, and the consistently elevated level of stress chemicals, can be devastating for children. It "shortens caps, called telomeres, which are chunks of DNA at the ends of chromosomes... and leads to premature cell aging," (Honig, 14) or, in other words, chronic stress causes a shortened lifespan.

Later in life, the elevation of childhood stress hormones leads to emotional problems, aggression, and even heart disease (Honig, 14-15). "Chaotic and hurtful childhoods lead to worrisome personality outcomes such as aggression and predatory violence in adulthood as well as drug abuse and victimization... Stresses in a child's life do not just add up; they multiply their worrisome effects... That is, after an individual reaches his or her stress threshold, there is a four-fold jump in developmental problems if more stresses are piled on the child" (Honig 15). So, while adults can often yoga or bar hop their way out of heightened stress levels, the entire well-being and lifespan of the child who experiences too much stress can be drastically diminished.

On the topic of shortened mortality rates and other impacts of stress and trauma, a psychological researcher at the Oregon Research Institute, shared with me in an interview:

> "Stressful life events in childhood can have large impacts on many domains of life, and these effects can last for decades. A good place to start in understanding the impact of early life trauma is the ACES study. ACES stands for 'Adverse Childhood Events.' This work uses a relatively simple measure, namely a count of how many adverse events a person has experienced in childhood. This is not very detailed, and yet this simple count predicts many life outcomes in adulthood, including risk of addiction, problems with employment, physical health problems, and mortality... Childhood betrayal traumas involve traumatic experiences where a child has experienced or witness[ed] a traumatic event for which a caregiver is responsible. They are thought to be especially impactful and damaging, because they involve the people a child depends on for their basic needs. So, these are areas where kids are at a great risk of harm."

[The psychologist asked to remain anonymous when he realized I wasn't able to share the entire interview, instead of just this portion.]

Simply put, keeping the stress levels in our children's lives low couldn't be much more important. That can be easier said than done for those who live in poverty, however, with all the stressors of too many bills to pay, low wages, high living expenses, subsequent poor diets and healthcare, and not enough money to make ends meet. In fact, "The Abecedarian Intervention Project, inspired by the Perry Preschool Study, illustrated how early intervention is critical in countering the environmental ramifications present in at-risk communities" (The Abecedarian Intervention Project). This study, conducted on 111 impoverished children, through the ages of infancy on to age five, produced fantastic evidence that early childhood intervention and education greatly reduces the consequences of growing up in poverty. The project showed, 20 years later, that children living in poverty who enter a quality daycare/preschool program –this one in particular, like most emerging philosophies on child development support, was "play-based, with a focus on language and cognitive development"- go on to have tremendously reduced rates of aggression, depression, violence, teen pregnancy, and jail time, and wonderfully increased levels of education, income, success, self-esteem, and general well-being.

In addition to providing a stimulating learning environment for our infants, toddlers, and preschoolers, we can help them build their own sense of internal resiliency. Resiliency is the ability to face and bounce back from challenges and adversity in life. According to Dr. Edith H. Grotberg on the International Resilience Project, we encourage a core sense of resilience in children by providing them with caring, reliable, stable caregivers, and using educational life experiences to show them how they are capable, trusted, lovable, autonomous, and responsible. As supportive and loving parents, we must give children tasks suited to their ages to help them see what they can do; we must care about how we function as role models in their lives; we must be affectionate, soothing, and consistent in our enforcing of rules. Children thrive when they know what we expect from them, what they can expect from us, and what they are capable of. A strong sense of self and bounce-back (resilience) is fundamental to a person's coping with life. And who doesn't believe in themselves more when the people who care about them clearly believe in them, too?

Obviously, a lot depends on how those first few formative years impact us. On a broader scale, Jean Bishop, Director of Early Childhood Education at Lane Community College, in Eugene Oregon, confirmed with me that development of the brain via quality experiences and interactions during the first several years of life is so critical that we absolutely must:

> "Advocate at the local, state and national level for quality care and for working conditions for parents that allow family to be a priority. Make sure all those in the field of ECE [early childhood education] have the education and training needed to guide children and offer curriculum

that is optimal for developing and enhancing emotion regulation, problem solving and peaceful conflict resolution. The early years are key and giving children the most loving, positive experiences possible in homes, schools and with their families will pay off in huge dividends later. This means our government must make the well-being of young children and their care a key national priority with funding available to back up this goal."

In accordance with this, there are also economists, like Dr. James Heckman, who insist that educating young ones saves taxpayers a lot of dollars in the future (by reducing dependence on welfare, prison sentences, etc.). It's time for people to understand the value in knowing how to best guide the youngest growing minds.

We plant a seed, after all, that grows every time we show a child she is lovable and respected as is, every time we give her new experiences that show her things she's capable of, every time we engage a toddler in a positive conversation or read him a good book, and every time we take a minute to ask ourselves how we'd like to be treated if we were the child in this moment. Additionally, it's important that they have age-appropriate experiences that support their stage of development, their self-esteem (self-love and self-worth), their budding sense and levels of competency, their safe curiosity and critical thinking skills, their trust in themselves and their parents, family members, and caregivers, their level of empathy and community, and a positive worldview.

Age-appropriate activities for infants include exploring and moving their bodies in a hazard-free space, listening to music, playing with rattles and sensory tubes, people singing to them, creating other soft sounds together, and adults mirroring their noises back to them in a friendly and caring manner, being read to, rolling balls, manipulating safe toys with their hands, experiencing both emotionally warm and lively environments, and calmer and quieter environments, being supported in self-soothing when they want the parent or caregiver to rush in and solve everything, and socializing with caring people. Older infants should have safe areas and items on which they can pull themselves up into a standing position, and push-toys with wheels that help them balance while they learn to walk.

Age-appropriate activities for toddlers include sensory projects (play-doh, shaving cream, rice and bean tables, water play, etc.), experimenting with musical instruments, songs, and rhythms, a lot of free time to explore artistically (painting with different types of paints, papers, brushes, sponges, etc.; using chalk, pastels, markers, etc.), dramatic play in which the adult sets up a themed area with resources (think restaurant with play food and menus, gas station with homemade box cars, animal wildlife safari, and more), block play for building and demolishing, learning to recognize letters, numbers, colors, shapes, and a lot of reading.

Age-appropriate activities for preschoolers, in addition to the above, include learning to cut and paste, learning to weave and string beads, learning to write those ABCs and numbers, learning phonetics, exploring cause and effect through simple science projects, having helper's chores around their home and child care program, honing their curiosity and critical thinking skills -in part by being encouraged to ask questions and join conversations, projects derived from the child's emerging interests, and the same dramatic play, musical play, art time, and reading as we give to our toddlers -aimed at their higher level of cognitive capacity, of course.

In addition to needing a wide array of quality experiences, children need a solid sense of emotional stability and consistency from the adults in their lives. Children thrive on the sense of security they feel when they know what to expect and what's expected of them. Children thrive knowing they are respected and valued (and adored, of course) for *who they are.* Children thrive knowing that when behaviors have to be corrected, this doesn't mean their parent thinks any less of them. These things improve their ability to trust in others, trust in themselves, and to relate positively to others with empathy. We develop attachment styles in childhood that make or break our relationships later in adulthood.

A lot has been written on the significance of the way our attachment styles affect our relationships with others later in adulthood. These attachment styles are developed in early childhood and they go on to impact all of our relationships for the rest of our lives. This is actually one of my favorite topics to teach people about because I believe our attachment styles affect us all, positively and negatively, incredibly deeply; adults should learn about attachment styles to improve our ability to have healthy relationships, setting better examples for our children, and to also help children develop their healthiest attachment styles from the very beginning.

The attachment styles include:

Secure attachment: the secure attachment is the ideal one. It's at the center of the spectrum of attachment styles, with insecure on one end and avoidant on the other. Insecure and avoidant are the two quite common extremes. Secure is the healthy, stable, and emotionally sound middle ground. This is where we want to help children be, in the way they relate and attach to people. The secure attachment responds in an even keel way to other people's feelings and needs, and to their own feelings and needs. It desires happiness and knows how to go about getting it and keeping it.

Insecure attachment: the insecure attachment is uncertain, clingy, jealous, and approval-seeking. It learned, somewhere early on, that it's only safe when it's receiving a lot of attention and devotion from its partner. It constantly fears rejection and abandonment. It expects the worst, even if just at the back of its mind. It regularly worries it isn't enough, isn't worthy of love, is going to be hurt and betrayed, is going to lose the one it loves, is going to have to give everything to keep/try to keep the one it loves, and often has emotional spin-outs when this

48

stress builds up too much. Insecure attachment sometimes (or often) victimizes itself in these ways.

We help these children by providing a strong sense of security and dependability. We show them we won't reject them for being themselves, that they don't have to earn our love and devotion to them, but that they intrinsically deserve love and respect. We help them learn to self-soothe and regulate themselves during their emotional storms and periods of overwhelming vulnerability and neediness. We help them learn a more secure attachment.

Avoidant attachment: the avoidant attachment is at the opposite end of the insecure attachment. Avoidant has learned that it's only safe when it's not relying on anyone, and not letting anyone get too close. Avoidant is afraid of intimacy, inter-dependence with another, and feeling like it's giving up its power by "giving in" to another person. Avoidant is self-centered in its drive to preserve its independence, even to the point of (even if unintentionally) using and then discarding other people. The partner to the avoidant type may only start to see the traits arise once an opportunity for commitment or "too much" intimacy has developed.

We help these children learn it's safe to work in partnership with each other, and safe to trust, depend on, and even need each other. We help them build empathy for others, not give up on others who show a need for them, and help them open up with us. The avoidant attachment can be difficult to heal; it's crucial that we help these children rebuild their ability to connect with others without going on to sabotage those connections by pushing people away.

An interesting fact about the insecure and avoidant attachment styles is that they attract each other and feed each other's fears of what to expect from people. Insecure people "prove" to the avoidant that it isn't safe for people to need anything from them, while avoidant people "prove" to the insecure that they aren't enough to keep someone around; they'll be pushed away. The insecure becomes more needy while the avoidant becomes more distant, and they sabotage the relationship. Another reason to encourage a more secure attachment style!

Avoidant-insecure attachment: as the name implies, this attachment style combines the characteristics of both avoidant and insecure. This person is needy, insecure, and doting over their loved ones, until they feel like someone needs too much or is getting too close. This person creates a strong (and unstable) push and pull of others in their relationships. We help these children by combining the ways of helping children listed above.

Earned secure attachment: we can relearn our attachment styles with self-reflection and awareness, and with good intentions and emotional regulation. We can help children relearn their attachment styles by disproving to them their fears about people: teaching insecure types that they won't be rejected or abandoned, and teaching avoidant types that they can trust relying on other people. We do this by using the methods listed previously, and by showing them our relationships with each other are safe.

I hope you'll look more into attachment styles and how to encourage secure attachments in children.

It's also quite powerful, of course, to be able to heal our own (or display our secure attachments from the beginning) and demonstrate healthy attachment styles as role models. Our children will follow our guidance and also mirror our actions, our relationships with others, and our personalities -including all of our strengths and weaknesses! They are sponges, constantly collecting information on "how to people," so let's give them the BEST input possible.

Children feel strengthened in their sense of security when they have their own belongings and their own spaces for such. In my home, we have things that we share *and* things that belong to an individual. Items of individuals are respected, and asking to use them is required. For example, if I buy a family treat, it's a free-for-all; if I buy someone an individual treat (or they come home with one) instead, we have to ask them for some, if we want some. The answer on sharing is up to the person whose treat it is. While sharing is an important quality to help foster in our children, forcing someone to share isn't the same experience as *choosing* to share. Respecting those boundaries helps children develops good boundaries themselves. If children know there's an important distinction between where they end and another family member begins (including their belongings), it will help them to also respect the boundaries of adults, and to continue to implement, expect, and nurture healthy boundaries as they grow into adulthood.

Additionally, a clean and safe environment is obviously the most conducive to a child's wellness. Furniture, outdoor equipment, dishes, toys, bedding, toilets, and anything else that children have contact with should be maintained in a safe and clean manner. This includes a clean fridge that holds their food, a clean dishwasher that washes their dishes, a clean mop-head which cleans their floors, etc. Children and adults should also wash hands regularly and often, clean up after themselves, take measures to prevent the spread of illnesses, and help each other clean up to support teamwork. Children should never be exposed to cleaning supplies, hazardous items, nor allowed to play with trash. Children deserve to live in safety and to learn how to create safety around them, as well.

Children also need a regular, consistent schedule. Even from birth -while infants must sleep and eat on their own schedule of tiredness and hunger/thirst, they develop routines for needing these things, and we are here to provide them with consistency. Like, an 8 month old child is usually going to need a morning nap and afternoon nap - parents should avoid waiting until the child is melting down tired before laying them down in bed. Children thrive much more happily when they know they can rely on a consistent routine. That doesn't mean the routine can't adapt -in fact it should! As the needs of the child change, so should what we provide them. The key is routine and consistency designed for a smoothly functioning day and family system.

Our daily schedule at home looks like this:

- 8:00 breakfast
- 8:30 read books, quiet play time

- 9:00 diaper changes, then nap for babies/art time for older kiddos
- 10:00 free play activities for older kiddos/outside play time
- 11:00/11:30 lunch
- 12:00 diapers, sensory activities
- 12:30/1:00 nap time for older kids/music and rattles, free play for babies
- 3:00 diapers
- 3:30 snack and second nap time for babies
- 4/4:30 outside play time
- 6:00 family dinner
- 8:00 bedtime

Finally, children need a regular, hefty amount of daily BONDING TIME! Snuggle, play, create things together, listen to their stories, show an interest in their imaginations and feelings and dreams, laugh together as often as possible, enjoy the small things in life, make and enjoy yummy and healthy foods together, talk about life (age-appropriately, please), hold them respectively and supportively when they're having hard feelings, rather than taking it personally or engaging with them as if they're an adult who has attacked or wronged you, talk to them sarcasm-free, and in a way that does not talk down to them, and support their interests in your time together!

We never get this time back with our children, once it has passed. Our focus should be on creating the best lives for them, and savoring every moment of it possible. When they're grown, every tone of voice we've used with them, every laughter or yelling match we've had, every word and hug and moment of closeness or separation has helped to *build who they are*, and has shaped their opinions of themselves and of us. Helping guide them in the most loving and strong light is more important than feeling right in a fight, or having the last word, or being frustrated that we've stepped on Legos for the 4,000th time. Our frustrated feelings are *our* problem, not theirs. Giving them the best response, as their parents, should be our biggest priority.

A final note on childhood stress is that we have innumerable tools available to assist children in regulating their stress levels: we can support them by creating a calm, safe, happy, and supportive environment, by keeping our own stress levels low enough to be able to focus on each person's individual needs and interests, by keeping our children engaged in activities and healthy conversation (or quiet, solo activities, when that's what they/we need instead) -instead of allowing boredom to creep in, by playing soft music, by putting calming scents like essential oils (natural, not artificial) into the air, by helping children learn to breathe or stretch or jump or hug through big feelings until they can talk it out, by being attentive and loving listeners (not trying to fix their problems FOR them, but working on and through things WITH them), by reflecting their feelings to them in speech (i.e. "Aww, my sweet child, you're sad today! I see this is making you very sad. What can I do to help? What do you need?"), and by modeling good communication skills for them to adopt, by parenting a family that plays happily and creatively together, and by setting up your home space in an open, warm, and comforting way. Let's talk next about what goes into stimulating, supportive, engaging, developmentally-appropriate activities to nourish the brains and imaginations of our kids. Let's look at the best way to set up our home play spaces and the learning opportunities that we provide for our children.

Children are incredible: they're intelligent, creative, resilient, and they want to make the most of their environments and connections with people. The space and resources we provide for them can make or break their learning and play experiences at home. Think about your favorite family member or teacher growing up compared to your least favorite. Do you see how the adult and the atmosphere made all the difference in your life? It's up to us, then, to remember that children need age-appropriate materials, experiences, and activities that are designed to encourage fun and learning, and that scaffold growth.

By creating the best atmosphere possible, we can give our children opportunities for growth and development through play and exploration. Maria Montessori said that play is the *work* of the child. This sentiment should not be underestimated! Childhood play can seem meaningless to many adults, but it's so much more than that to children. It's how they mimic and process the world around them. It's how they practice being people in new ways. It's how they begin to explore, connect the dots, and most actively and directly learn from their environments. Play becomes the best kind of knowledge: experiential knowledge, or knowing through doing. Play encourages development in all areas: physical, cognitive, language, and socio-emotional.

Questions from adults can go a long way to scaffold a child's learning and exploration, by getting them to think and connect the dots in new ways. These should be questions that we don't answer for them, like, "What will happen if you _____" and "What do you think should happen next?" "How can you make that happen?" "How did you decide to do that?" "What would have made that different?" Etc. We can do this when our kids are creating art, building with Legos or magnetic tiles, creating narratives, and any time we'd like to stimulate their thought process and imagination.

Peer-influenced and adult-supported play can help push a child out of their "zone of proximal development" (or ZPD). The ZPD refers to a child's readiness and ability to grow beyond their current zone or level of development. Play can nudge a child to develop new skills, and build new understandings. It's children learning to cut with safety scissors after watching their older sibling do it successfully, or learning to assemble jigsaw puzzles -this is cognitive growth. It's realizing that the way they play can impact the feelings of the people around them for better or for worse, and their relationships with those people -this is socio-emotional growth. It's learning that they can safely climb higher than they used to, or jump farther -this is physical/gross motor growth.

From the Simply Psychology website, Saul McLeod writes,

> The concept, "Zone of Proximal Development" (ZPD) was developed by Soviet psychologist and social constructivist Lev Vygotsky (1896 – 1934). The ZPD refers to the difference between what a learner can do without help and what he or she can achieve with guidance and encouragement from a skilled partner. Thus, the term "proximal" refers to those skills that the learner is "close" to mastering.

The zone of proximal development (ZPD) has been defined as: "the distance between the actual developmental level as determined by independent problem solving and the level of potential development as determined through problem-solving under adult guidance, or in collaboration with more capable peers" (Vygotsky, 1978, p. 86). Vygotsky believed that when a student is in the ZPD for a particular task, providing the appropriate assistance will give the student enough of a "boost" to achieve the task.

So, it is our goal, as parents and role models, to give our children nudges of support that help them move themselves into the next zone of their development. We don't let them figure it all out on their own, nor do we do the work for them. We give them a balanced, supportive nudge in the right direction and *help them help themselves*. Part of parenting is being here to observe their current capacities, and support their movement into new zones of development by nudging their exploration of themselves, their environment, and their own skills. We further assist this process via repetition and practice. Children do, do, do and then eventually realize they can now do more than before. We help facilitate this, or fail to, depending on the quality of attention we provide them, and by the quality of play activities we provide for them.

What is "developmentally-appropriate," or "age-appropriate?" These terms mean that the activities and materials are right for the development and/or age of the child. Typically developing children (compared to someone who is developing atypically: more delayed, or with a disability) tend to fall into categories of development by age group. Thus, we have newborns, infants, wobblers, toddlers, preschoolers, school-aged children, and all the different developmentally-appropriate activities for each group. (This section is only written for up to preschool age because that's my area of expertise. There are fantastic resources all over the internet and in bookstores for older children, though!)

Newborns mainly need a safe, loving, nurturing environment to sleep, be held, be fed, be changed, be kept clean, and be kept at a healthy temperature. The newborn is never too young for us to hold eye contact, smile at them, and use (and demonstrate) language in a warm and loving tone of voice.

Infants -around 2 to 12 months old- additionally need a safe space to move their limbs, begin to crawl and sit and pull themselves up and start taking steps. They need toys that won't pop small, choking pieces into their mouths. They need to hear and see books and songs and language in use! They need us to interact kindly, patiently, and joyfully with them, the older ones enjoying playing clapping games, peek-a-boo, shaking rattles, and putting EVERYTHING in their mouths (something to be very careful about).

Children begin to learn now, in the first few years of their lives, whether they'll get their needs met by being either whiny, domineering, or reasonable. It's our responses to them that either enable or deny them, in their endeavors and growth. It's the responsibility of their caregivers to help them find the best approach and most secure route of learning how to get their needs supported.

Wobblers -around 10 to 14 months through two years old- want a lot of interaction from their parents, lots of repetition which helps pave neural pathways, to play alongside other children rather than engaged with them (they don't have the cognitive capacity/brain development for that just yet), to grab everything, mouth everything, to begin developing their fine motor skills like using their "pincer grab" for things like picking up cheerios, and to begin walking, and then running. Wobblers need a lot of supervision! Wobbler is the perfect term because these newly walking babies tend to wobble and fall down a lot. Yet they're finally mobile, so they want into everything! They need constant supervision, soft toys without any choking hazards, toys that make noise, toys for stacking and combining, toys with wheels, board books, they can start painting, they will have been understanding your language for a while now, and will be repeating the words they hear most often, hungry to learn more and communicate as much as possible. They need opportunities for safe running, throwing balls, going for walks, and a couple of naps each day. Naps should be consistent, around the same time each day! To develop a sense of capability, wobblers can start learning to put toys away in boxes/cubbies, to wash their own hands and table area with a washcloth after eating, to hand you food they don't want instead of throwing it on the floor, and to say please and thank you.

Children this young in my home-based preschool child care program (my profession of almost 20 years) LOVE to watch me teaching the older kids. In fact, without fail they grow up loving to learn and knowing ABCs, numbers, colors, songs, and so much more way sooner than other children their age. You can implement this kind of learning this young even when it seems they may not get it; it fosters a love of learning that is an advantage to them, and that tends to stay with them as they grow up.

Toddlers -around 2 to 3 years old- are very active, are mastering their ability to run, have a large vocabulary and talk a lot, and have moved onto one mid-day nap. These sweet ones should be starting/continuing to learn their ABCs, colors, shapes, numbers, counting, animals, etc. (they may have also started these things as a wobbler, if someone is helping them learn). They are interested in learning to match things up and put things together (like shapes through shape holes in a box, or large and simple puzzles), they can start learning with help how to string beads, they should be enjoying sensory play activities (still looking out for choking hazards at this age), they will sing along to the many songs you've been singing to them now, and will love to dance, jump, run, climb, put big mega-bloks together, race cars, hold baby dolls and pretend to feed them. They may start engaging in play with peers instead of only playing on their own or alongside them.

When that begins, you can start introducing buddy games that require teamwork. To develop a sense of capability, toddlers can scrape their meal plates into the trash or compost, can wash their faces, hands, and table area with a washcloth after eating, can be learning to wash their hands in the sink, can be working on potty-training (taking their undies up and down on their own is a big one), putting their own coat and shoes on to go outside, sweeping with a child size broom -or pretending to, putting toys and books back on shelves and in cubbies or boxes, and helping put food ingredients into a pan or bowl for making meals.

Preschoolers -around 3 to 4 years old for younger preschoolers, and 4 to 5 years old for older preschoolers- these kids love learning! They are soaking everything up, all the time! They are asking "Whhyyy?" a *lot* because the critical thinking area of their brains and cognitive capacities are finally ready to question *everything* in the attempt of understanding all things and connecting all the dots. This is a very significant step (and tool) toward cognitive development and them becoming competent in thinking for themselves! They also *love* feeling capable and independent, and want to be in charge of themselves (and maybe others) whenever possible. They've learned they can negotiate with parents and have some say in how their lives are impacted. They may begin experimenting with power plays, bluffing, manipulating, and lying. It's important to allow them a sense of autonomy while also teaching them to be honest, trustworthy, responsible people.

The social interaction experience with family members and friends explodes in this age group! Children want to bond with each other, pick fights with each other, be best friends with each other, create unlimited fictional worlds of play and art together, and on their own; they want to play family, play restaurant, play doctor, play princesses and pirates... they want to explore relationships and make believe with each other in every way!

If possible, in the home, this age group should have plenty of free play time allowed to them, with a dramatic play area for dress up, with a mirror or two, with baby dolls, with pretend food, etc., and with space for making forts, and for building imaginary worlds, sometimes on their own and other times with other family members.

This group also needs the most variety of learning activities, now that their skills are taking off in every direction: tracing ABCs, practicing phonetics, connecting sounds to learn to read and write, counting, adding, tracing numbers, recognizing and creating patterns, mastering puzzles and mazes, a variety of regular art projects and freestyle art time, sensory play like play-doh and shaving cream and kinetic sand, etc., daily reading time, lots of outside play and optional outdoor games, exploring nature, flash cards, beading, stamps and ink play, dancing, playing instruments, science experiments, gardening, cooking, learning to help clean up, and so much more. Their sense of capability will come from going potty on their own, washing their hands by themselves, scraping their dishes and cleaning up their eating area, being involved in cooking and baking, helping wash dishes, throwing things in the trash, cleaning up toys, getting out and putting away their nap time bedding, helping in the garden with instruction, helping wash the dog or brush the cat, etc. Give them simple responsibilities that they see grownups doing all the time!

Our ability to provide play areas is going to vary depending on the amount of space we have for the children, of course. Most of us may only have one corner of our child's bedroom to work with. An excellent way to work around that is to have a table that children can work at where the activities change. While we do painting, sensory play, play-doh, puzzles, curriculum activities like tracing and writing and counting objects, and stringing beads at the same table where we eat, your child can also have a table in their room that is sometimes a block building table, sometimes a race car and train track table, sometimes a restaurant, sometimes a tea party, sometimes a doctor's office, an exploration table for items from nature, etc. This table could be turned into their Post Office, or Grocery Store. The options are endless. One blank table can revolve as many types of play areas! Maybe it changes daily, weekly, or even daily. Just remember that children typically get a bigger benefit from having plenty of time to explore something, rather than by only having a limited time. Children get the most out of something if they can use and explore it until they grow bored with it. Then onto what's next!

In our child's play activities, we want to be encouraging growth in all their domains of development:

Socio-emotional: this is social and emotional, or how they form healthy friendships and relationships, how they mimic parenting with dolls, build self-esteem, develop self-soothing mechanisms, how they communicate, and how they learn to regulate their own feelings.

Cognitive: the ability to comprehend, calculate, format thoughts, form deductive reasoning and critical thinking skills, and general intellectual awareness. Think learning from observing, recognizing patterns, and understanding things in new, broadened ways.

Language: this includes literacy. Many argue that strong language and literacy skills can empower a child through life more than learning any other subject at school will, because a love of reading and language will help them continue to learn throughout their entire lives. This area of play, and associated activities, supports reading, writing, developing stories, learning new languages, improved vocabulary, and singing.

Physical: both gross motor skills and fine motor skills. Gross motor skills, or large motor skills, are things like running, jumping, climbing, throwing, and kicking. Fine motor skills include being able to pick up cheerios with your pinching fingers, threading beads, writing letters, and using tools. Sensory play also falls into this category. Children learn *so much* through their senses!

Remember that the areas we are about to discuss will vary and change depending on the ages and developmental abilities of your children. A one year old is typically going to be working on the domains of development in a much simpler way than a four year old will, for example. While an infant may mostly want space to safely learn to crawl and walk, an older child will typically want more options for running, jumping, climbing, stomping, throwing, catching, dancing, etc.

I find that socio-emotional support, specifically, is required at all times with young children! It plays into our every moment: I help my children learn good manners, how to communicate peacefully and assertively, how to be in touch with their own feelings, how to be conscious and empathetic toward others' feelings, respectful of their own boundaries *and* others' boundaries, and how to be accountable and responsible for their own emotions, reactions, and needs. Younger children are learning not to grab and take things from people, not to throw tantrums to get what they want, and how to ask for help. They often need help working out boundaries and how to get their needs met during most of their interactions with each other. This helps them build their ability to have relationships and ability to take care of themselves in regards to other people.

Activities that encourage socio-emotional development do so by encouraging teamwork or by allowing for more than one person to play, hopefully interactively with siblings, parents, or friends: the drama and dress up corner, the puppet show zone, the baby and kitchen/house area, and other role-playing areas like the hospital, the post office, the grocery store, and the zoo.

Cognitive activities will support learning about math, science, and understanding things more complexly. This can be explored on a light table, during activities like counting, adding, subtracting, by doing science experiments and discussing what may or may not happen and why, and practicing new skills such as cutting and pasting, tracing and writing, and different types of puzzles, etc. Cognitive development is encouraged during listening, in response to questions, educational videos, and even story time when children learn new things and are allowed to ask questions and converse about new topics.

Language activities and areas can include a reading corner full of books, big comfy pillows and carpeting, plus pictures of children reading on the wall. They can be a table with chairs near an alphabet poster on the wall that offers paper and pens for your children to practice writing. It can be the area where music gets turned on for children and adults to sing along (and dance?). It can be all of the above. Older children can "write" and decorate their own books to be put on display or to send to family members as presents. Notebooks and tracing books can be kept here to pull out when it's writing practice time. Even two year old toddlers can enjoy this experience, especially when they see their older preschool and school-aged siblings enjoying "writing like grown-ups."

Physical areas include both indoor and outdoor spaces. Aside from our family garden, I like to have my back yard set up entirely for gross motor play: big cars for driving in, bikes for riding on, a slide for climbing and going down, a large grassy area for racing and kicking balls, and throwing and catching balls -though we do also have some fine motor activities out there, too, like chalk for the sidewalk, and bubbles for blowing. Inside isn't the best area for our gross motor activities because it's full of furniture, our belongings, and our big kitchen table (where we eat and do a lot of activities). But we do still have physical activity time indoors, like dancing the hokey pokey, racing back and forth, zooming the big trucks around, and jumping on the small one-person trampoline because physical activity is extremely important for good physical health, good mental health, and for longevity. Obviously, many people can't afford homes that provide large fenced yards. That's what bike rides and trips to the park are for! Riding bikes and going to the park with my mom and little sister are some of my favorite childhood memories!

Our lives are becoming increasingly more and more sedentary, a habit that has been proven over and over to be linked to poor health and shortened lifespans. Physical activity not only keeps us at our physically healthiest -along with good nutrition, good hydration, proper sleep, and less stressful lifestyles- but also regulates our hormones and the chemicals our brains produce -an important aspect of good mental health. Using our bodies regularly, and knowing their strength and capability, is also key in being able to trust our physical forms as we get older. People who grow up regularly using and strengthening their bodies tend to have more confidence in what they can do in their lives.

We spend a lot of time every day sitting down to eat, sleeping, sitting in a car or on a bus, sitting down to read, work, and do other quiet activities, and sitting down to watch TV or use electronics; it's very important to use our bodies actively in between these things! This clearly applies mostly to those of us with full use of our bodies, but most differently-abled bodies can build strength and flexibility, too. The benefits to our health are too great to ignore! Children deserve the healthiest start possible.

In Oregon, the state child care division mandates that providers caring for young children may allot only two hours of electronic time to the children each day. I have found, in my own business, that if your curriculum is active and stimulating, two hours each day is a LOT of TV/electronics time! My child care kids typically watch an educational video, related to our monthly themes, while lunch is made. We also currently have movie day on Fridays where we can use the full two hours, or close to it, unless they decide they'd rather play (which they usually do).

If you have young children in child care, though, are they getting two hours of TV time there *and* coming home to more electronics time? If you have young children at home with you instead, are they spending a lot of time on the TV to make your day a little easier? If you have older children at home, are you participating in the common practice of watching TV all night after both school and work are over?

Kids love learning via electronics and love being entertained by them. Electronics are alluring, stimulating, and hard to ignore. They can give parents (and child care providers who are working 10-12+ hours per day) a well-needed break from the constant attention and devotion we provide so often, on top of all the other daily demands of life. And electronics can teach children in additional ways to what we bring to the table. They CAN have valuable benefits, when used properly. The top three important factors are, then,

1.) What's the quality of what they're watching? It's our job to create the best influence for our children, and protect them from the negative stuff, which includes screening materials to be age-appropriate. I'd also argue that we must look for resources that are educational, that are positive and uplifting (as much as possible), and that encourage integrity and empathy. We don't want our kids watching outdated tropes that paint women and girls as weak, for example. Or that display too much conflict. We do want to use this time to guide them to be great people, even if indirectly. If we're going to rely on electronic time, the content should be high quality and have a good impact on the kids watching it.

2.) How do we further scaffold their learning via electronics? Whether it's a movie, an educational video on YouTube, or a LeapFrog learning toy, we can take what the kids are learning to the next level by discussing things they saw and learned. We can observe which topics our children seem most interested in and dive further into our understanding of those topics by researching them online, picking up related books from the library, maybe even attending a related class with our kiddos, or going on a family field trip. This also personalizes the electronic teaching/learning experience. It brings it back to the people in the family. Furthermore, children *love* questions, and questions encourage their thinking and reflecting skills; we can ask what they thought of _____ that they heard/saw/learned; what did they like and dislike; what do they think would've happened differently if _____? Etc.

3.) How much time do we allow kids to use electronics? Researchers and experts agree that children under the age of two shouldn't even be exposed to a screen. Their brains are developing so quickly that they need human interaction *as often as possible*. They need to be saturated with quality, non-electronic experiences, like experiencing intimate eye contact and facial expressions, being held, being played with, being talked to, being shown things in the world, us mirroring their faces and speech and feelings (mirroring, not mocking, of course), singing, reading stories, going to the park, eating together, and other personal interactions. If you're skeptical about the importance of limiting electronics time, you can do a quick internet search and you'll see that the American Pediatric Association, and many others, say to limit electronic time to two hours a day at the most! And many are concerned that that's actually too much time.

It's clear to me that we're moving into the Age of Technology. Children should therefore not be denied the ability to be technologically savvy in such a time! It may possibly *be* the key to their productive future, being in the know. However, young children are now spending a lot of time witnessing their parents glued to a smartphone, a computer or tablet, and a television. They are getting the influence of social programming to live on those things just by being alive and part of society. This is out of balance with the rest of life, and what is natural for mammals.

So, although it makes perfect sense for older children to know how to type and read code and work electronics, and maybe desire to grow up and improve upon our technology, younger children should have more protective guidelines given to them. Two hours a day of TV, for example, means two more hours a day spent sitting and sedentary; it means two whole hours of not reading, playing, exploring, bonding with peers and loved ones, painting, making music, running outside, jumping on a small trampoline inside, working on puzzles, tracing ABCs to learn to write, learning to cook, learning to garden, and the list goes on. There are so many other, better things children can be doing and learning in that time!

If we need to include that time in our daily schedule, though -and parents do have their reasons, an alternative is to break up the electronic time throughout the day. We can have electronics on for shorter periods, like 20 minutes, while younger children must wait patiently for mom to take a shower. Or while dinner is made for 30 minutes, if this is a task the child can't help with. Or perhaps your older child earns an hour of electronic time in the evening for having completed their chores and homework. Or would it work for you to play 20 minutes a day of videos or video games that your kids would want to jump, dance, and sing to, to help them get more physically active in a way they enjoy? Or 20 minutes a day at nap time of calming videos to help children relax into their beds? Or 20 minutes of both? Maybe your family has a weekend movie night, so you limit weekly use of TV and electronics?

I have found, time and time again, in my 20 years of raising my children and working to care for and teach other people's children, that because of the way TV alters our brain waves, it also alters our moods. Kids watching too much TV, playing too many video games, or being exposed to other electronics for too long -just like an adult who has to look at a computer screen all day- end up feeling frazzled, moody, and depleted by the experience. I'm pretty certain, as well, that when we're old and nearing the ends of our lives, we won't look back and wish we had watched more TV.

Our bodies are designed to move! Our bodies are designed to develop strength and speed, and to pursue a healthy and successful survival. While this may not apply as much to children who are physically developing atypically, or who live with disabilities, physical movement however we can incorporate it into our lives is extremely crucial and beneficial to our health. Getting our blood pumping is part of regulating the chemicals and hormones that affect our moods, it's part of circulatory and heart health, it's necessary for properly pushing toxins and cellular waste through our lymphatic systems, it's good for our lungs and for oxygenating our entire bodies, it builds muscle which makes for stronger bones, and it assists in adequate digestion, absorption, elimination, and metabolism. It also teaches children physical competency, and helps them to "be in their bodies," compared to dissociating due to stress (and/or trauma). Physical activity helps them know and trust their own bodies, learn to push their own limits and grow, and supports them being in touch with themselves on a physical level.

Physical activity has been proven to be the key to longevity! It strengthens us in ways we deserve to know as early on in life as possible; it helps create our healthiest bodies and greatly enhances our mental health. By providing our children with quality nutrition via their daily meals and snacks, encouraging healthy and happy relationships with food, offering a holistically balanced and supportive environment, and guiding our children in regular daily physical activity and fitness, we can give these kids their best start possible. So, let's get up and get out there and make quality life experiences while we can! Face to face, hand in hand, heart to heart. This is how we thrive!

Parenting, clearly, is an interesting mix of providing challenging activities for our children, protecting them while still helping them build a solid core of resilience to life's downfalls and hurdles, and supporting their socio-emotional development and health. The foundation of their sense of self and self-love will revolve around building strong self-esteem, self-efficacy, and empathy toward others. Though it may sound strange that relating to and caring for others (empathy) would enrich our own sense of self, our character and heart are deepened by being wired to support our fellow humans. Caring about more than just ourselves takes us a looong way in this world, and failing to develop altruism and empathy stunts our growth and well-being.

We cannot be strong leaders, strong partners, strong parents, strong caregivers, strong doctors, strong teachers, strong friends, strong neighbors, strong politicians, nor *anything else,* for that matter, if we do not have a heart that cares for the well-being of others. We *must* be able to understand, empathetically, what it's like to stand in another's shoes, and to walk another's path of existence, for us to have a well-rounded consciousness and perspective on life. We cannot seek a peaceful future, we cannot seek harmonious communications, and reliable relationships without a sense of caring for others. Without a sense of caring for others, we have nothing of value to offer them. It's a lonely, shallow, confusing existence to be self-absorbed and find that the entire world does not bow to your every whim. That's because life is meant to be lived in harmony with others. Even our personal relationships exist within an ecosystem. We either nourish them properly, or they fail us.

Lucky for us, deepening our capacities for caring about others, expands our own capacity for self-love and self-respect. Empathy is a two-way street. Even when it isn't returned by others, it grows kind morals within us that enrich our life and our sense of purpose and value. When children learn to see that we're all in this together, what they seek to bring to the table of life drastically changes. Cognitively, their brains will be wired to have them inclined to see themselves as the center of their universe until their late teens. To encourage the fostering of empathy otherwise, though, we can:

- Set healthy boundaries whose purposes are clear to the child.
- Respect the child's boundaries, and model respectful behavior elsewhere in life.
- Check with them to see how they are feeling, why, and what they need when they are upset, instead of reacting with our own negative emotions.
- Teach them to ask if their friends are okay, instead of forcing them to say sorry (when they've done something that upset a friend).
- Teach them to slow down and pay attention to the people, moods, and the general needs of the room or their environment.

- Teach them that their fears and big feelings are supported with kindness, patience, and the valuing of them for who they are. Then expect them to respond to others this way as well.
- Teach them to avoid harming anyone, and to avoid violence.
- Teach them concern and support for others rather than laughing at people who are hurt; rather than *provoking* people to feel hurt.
- Show them that vulnerability is strength. It's humble, it's open, it's in tune with feelings.

There are so many small gestures we can make to model empathy and altruism to our children. Altruism is helping someone who's dropped something, taking actions of paying it forward, wherein we do something kind and "for no reason," just to do something nice and show people there is good in the world. People can then pay that forward by doing something nice for "no reason" for someone else. Altruism is feeding the hungry, donating to important causes, sheltering the homeless, voting *for the people,* and the like.

This helps create a kinder world for those of us who are highly sensitive and emotionally gifted, as well. I often wonder if these two things go hand in hand with having a slow-to-warm temperament. In my experience working with children (and in being all three of the above: emotionally gifted, highly sensitive, and slow to warm; in addition to raising a child who is all these things, too), these characteristics often play out together. Usually, the child who is uncomfortable in new environments, around new people, or with changes to their routine, has a wide bubble in which they take everyone in, pick up on the essence of a new person's character and intentions, notice the undercurrents of a person's messages, and process feelings more intensely. When they are surrounded by people who seem unfazed by the constant onslaught of overstimulation and mixed messages, it's often overstimulating and confusing to the child: they know they are different (in this very significant way), but don't know how nor why.

Highly sensitive children, slow-to-warm children, and emotionally gifted children are, in fact, often at a disadvantage in larger groups where they don't have the saving graces of trust, consistent routines, trustworthy intimacy within the group, and the security of being bonded to a safe main caregiver. Children in general deserve a smaller group/class size wherein they receive patient and attentive kindness on a regular basis. So, let's talk about the differences between a quality in-home child care program versus daycare centers. First, let me explain the varying categories as I know them.

- **Nannies.** Nannies are paid minimum wage or higher (and taxes *are* required to be taken out on them. For your safety, see the IRS' website on this, if you are unaware that families must pay taxes on nannies as employees [unless you've hired the nanny via a

77

company that already pays the taxes on them]) to work in your home with just your children and family. Sometimes, they're happy to also serve as your housekeeper, cook, and chauffeur for errands and after-school activities. It depends on each individual nanny. They are an expensive option, as they deserve to make a living wage for their work, and are also the most personal option. Your child will have one-on-one care with a nanny. They also miss out on the socializing that comes from growing up in a child care setting. Hopefully, your nanny is educated in baby care and early childhood education.

- **Family Care.** Your child stays with a family member while you work. Chances are their caregiver doesn't have training in education and child development, and can't offer an enriching curriculum and quality socialization for your child. However, your child is comfortable (hopefully!) knowing they're with family.

- **"Exempt" Status Child Care.** This person is NOT registered by the state, is therefore not required to follow the rules and standards of the state, and is not monitored by anyone. They are legally required to have a much smaller group of children.

- **Registered Child Care.** This is a home-based child care program that is registered with the state in which you reside to be a safe place for children. These programs must pass a lot of requirements, certifications, and inspections by the state. You can review your Child Care Division's standards by doing an internet search or calling them. Registered care has the capacity for a large group of children at one time. It's often only one provider (or maybe them and their spouse) caring for the children all day, every day.

- **Certified Child Care.** This is a home-based child care program that meets far higher standards for care. It takes a LOT more to become certified with the state than it does to be registered. Certified programs are more school-like than registered ones. Consequently, they can have double or triple the size of children -and often employ assistant teacher staff members.

- **Certified Centers.** These are daycare centers, sometimes advertised as schools. They have multiple class rooms, many teachers and staff members, cooks, janitors, a landscape crew, an assistant director, and more. The student to teacher ratio is its most expanded in this setting. A preschool teacher may have 10 in one class. Often these classes have two teachers and 20 preschool aged children, to maximize the profits for the owner of the center.

As you're aware of by now, I've worked with young children for going on 20 years. It's one of my greatest joys in life! Most of that time has been spent running a full-time preschool child care business from home, while I raised my own family and slowly but surely finished my degree with an extra year's focus in child development and education. A couple of those years, however, were spent working as a teacher in some daycare centers, here in town. After my almost 20 years of experience, I can't say that home-based programs and large centers are even close to equals. I've learned a lot about the contrasts between them.

Some families will prefer the environment of a daycare center to an in-home child care program; maybe they like the feeling of an established business or school better than a new person's home. Maybe they feel like it's easier to trust with so many professionals in the building, or they appreciate the academic setting. Maybe they want their baby exposed to a fast-paced environment with a lot of new people from the very beginning. Maybe they feel the employees will be held to a higher standard than you'd find in a home child care. However, new parents often don't know where to even begin, especially if they have no inside experience as a teacher/provider themselves. And a lot of families don't know the difference between centers and more personal home-based programs. While arguments can be made against *bad* child care, I'm specifically addressing *high quality* in-home child care programs, here, compared to daycare centers.

This account is, of course, just based on my own personal experience. That experience and perspective is a thorough one, though, as I have almost two decades of time running a very successful home business, have a degree in early learning and child development, "interned" at our college's high quality center while in school, worked as a teacher for Head Start, and have worked in both the worst center *and* best center here in my town. I've also spoken with dozens of child care families AND center/preschool co-workers over the past 15 years. The issues I have seen with each center/preschool -compared to quality in-home care- are these:

THE PAY TEACHERS RECEIVE

Daycare centers here charge $1200 - $1500 for infants, "wobblers," toddlers, and preschoolers, yet staff members are often only paid *minimum wage* or something barely above it, even though they typically give *sooo much* to their work. Employees are often required to have a degree in child development, and are then only paid $10 - $12 an hour. Those are poverty wages! *Especially* if the teacher has their own kids, student loans, medical expenses, and are

81

additionally paying for continuing education hours every year (done in their spare time), as required by law, etc. Meanwhile, the owner has enrolled 8-20 children at this the above tuition amount and is making a KILLING in PROFITS. As an employer myself, I know it's expensive to have staff. I also know it's worth it to pay them a good wage and be able to sleep at night, *still making a good living myself.* If I can do this with only eight to ten families in my care, big centers can do at least as much. Once the school or center reaches a certain number of students, the dozens more that enroll create pure profits. A bigger center is *the best* business model for the income of the person who owns it.

As a child care provider, however, I can charge parents far less, have a small happy group of well-attended-to kiddos, and actually make a living wage. Having eight children in my care equates to an income of about $7000 a month. Registered with the state, I can provide meals on the USDA Food Program (which I do anyway) and be reimbursed for a portion of the cost of their organic meals. I can actually support my family, and continue to enjoy what I do! It's a win for everyone here. Certified, instead of registered, I have found, I can have more children, pay an excellent teacher and assistant teacher good wages, give paid vacation and holiday time off, and make a good living. This keeps us enjoying our work, loving what we do, and feeling valued for everything we give all day.

SICK POLICIES

Daycare center teachers are expected to work sick. If they go home throwing up, they're expected back the next day —instead of 24 hours after vomiting has subsided, like the state licensing facility mandates. Children usually aren't sent home sick, either, unless they're throwing up with a very high fever. I've seen cases of pink eye, diarrhea, bronchitis, and influenza get passed around a classroom for an entire month or more because sick children (and teachers) are kept in care! Some families will prefer not having to come pick up their sick child and miss work, but most of the people I know have told me directly that they want to know if their baby needs a doctor or needs to go home.

In a quality home-based child care program, contagious children go home/stay home, as mandated by state law. If the provider becomes too sick to work, they will often have a substitute that everyone knows, likes, and trusts who can come and cover them. And if no substitute is available, when s/he falls ill, families will be reimbursed for the sick day. In my experience, providers typically get sick a LOT less often, and recover more quickly, when sick children are staying home until they're over their illnesses. It's smart for parents to always have their own, trusted back up care, or back up plan, for emergencies and sick days, just in case!

RATIOS: THE NUMBER OF TEACHERS AND CHILDREN

Ratios are maxed out in the classrooms at centers. Meaning directors will usually structure their small classrooms to have as many children in them as possible, with as few teachers as possible. That makes the owner the biggest profit. With preschoolers, that might mean 18 or 20 four year old children are packed into one small, very busy and noisy classroom with only two overworked and underpaid teachers. But for younger children, the infants and wobblers, that typically means eight babies, in a small room, with two teachers, where they spend a large part of their day crying, and fighting for a caregiver's attention. These babies are typically shuffled from one feeding, diaper-changing, and being rocked to sleep, to the next, until all eight babies have had their basic needs met. And then that cycle starts all over again, while the babies scream for the attention of the adults. If a child is crying during the routine, maybe because they are new to the classroom and experiencing attachment issues, because they're used to being held all the time and don't want to share their care provider, because the room has other new children who are also crying and screaming a lot, because they're not used to seeing seven other sets of parents dropping a child off, because they've had six different staff members come into their room today to give the two teachers their breaks, etc... they are often left to "cry it out" because there is so much work to be done for eight babies and only two adults. (Even just reducing the ratio from 8:2 to 4:1 [or 3:1, ideally] and introducing one new child at a time, reduces the stress levels of this kind of classroom drastically!)

On top of this, daycare workers don't have a say over who is in their classroom. Preschoolers who have been telling their peers how they're going to murder them (it happens), for example, or toddlers who are punching and biting without improvement to their behavior, and babies who clearly need one-on-one care are often all allowed to stay, no matter the detriment caused to them, the rest of the children, and the environment. I've seen a lot of teachers quit their jobs over this. (*To be fair, I have seen some classrooms that function far better than others; the space is large with a smaller group of children, and is really well-designed to support the interests of the children, with a developmentally appropriate curriculum. They are not ALL chaotic for the children. So many other classes, though, aren't as well-supported. And those are the ones in that just aren't the best for our kids.)

As an in-home care provider, I'm very careful about who the innocent babies and children in my care are exposed to. I'm very careful about keeping our group a safe, kind, and happy one. Child care providers have an entirely different requirement for ratios than classrooms do, too. You should check with your local child care division for the specifics. In Oregon, a registered in-home provider can have up to six children who are too young to be in school, and only two of those being younger than two years old. While some providers have older kids around after school –often their own- usually the child care group

85

during the day consists of only six young children, or fewer. BONUS: child care providers decide for themselves if they only want four children, or two children, or six children, compared to being forced to take the maximum amount that the center wants them to have. *Can you imagine the difference between a room of six thriving preschoolers compared to 18 bored or aggravated ones?*

CONSISTENCY, ROUTINE, AND SENSE OF SECURITY

Sadly, there's a lot of inconsistency and flux in centers. Children get moved, every few months, to a new classroom as they get older. Not only are young children exposed to multiple teachers, and the adults giving those teachers breaks, or covering them if they're out for a day, but they're regularly exposed to children leaving and new, scared children starting. I worked in one place where we had FIVE new babies start within two weeks *–many of those parents and children never even met us teachers first-* and they and the other children were pretty terrified and miserable for quite a while. Then children get moved to the next class and go through the process all over again.

In addition, with the level of overworked and underpaid burn out that happens to teachers of young children, there's a really high turnover rate in the preschool and daycare center industry. Babies and children in centers, have to emotionally grapple with having attachments (or lack of attachments) to their caregivers who don't stay in their lives for very long.

For all of these reasons, I've come to believe that daycare centers are usually a very unsettling environment for most young children. They will do their best to adapt, as we all do, but they won't thrive as well as they otherwise could.

In a quality home-based program, however, the child care provider is typically the child's main caregiver and teacher, for *years!* And the children get to know us very well. We probably also have an assistant or substitute. New children are usually only introduced one or two at a time, to allow them time to adjust, and keep everyone there thriving comfortably. The program, ideally, will be structured around the children, *rather than the adults and the profit potential,* meaning we get to know each child and their needs, and adjust the curriculum as necessary. We can observe their temperaments and attachment styles and adjust accordingly. Feisty children can learn more empathy, slow-to-warm children can learn trust and emotional bravery, and easy-going children can learn to stand up for themselves better (safely learn to not be *too* easy going), etc.

With younger children, there is a much greater sense of safety and care found in having a regular routine, with other peers who are well-adjusted to being there, instead of a lot of new faces coming and going, nothing unexpected from the environment, and FAR more time for us to engage with the children, soothe them, guide them, and create awesome opportunities for positive socio-emotional experiences, exploring creativity and imagination, developing quality relationships with each other, fostering trust and capability, and so much more! The question is, how do you want your child socialized?

87

VISIBILITY

The greatest strength for parents, in my opinion, of a daycare center over an in-home program is the visibility. Having a lot of co-workers and constant in-and-out of families can help some employees remain accountable for their behavior. Technically, there are more eyes on your child, and the employees. And this kind of social environment also creates a sense of moral support for teachers -in better centers, anyway. Employees can learn from each other, rely on each other, etc.

However, visibility isn't always assured, and is sometimes sold as something it's not. It's not uncommon for some lower quality child care centers to be found employing teachers who aren't teacher qualified by the state's mandates, or that have gotten in trouble for having employees that were aggressive with the children, or to have teachers who cover up their co-workers' or boss' mistakes. This isn't always the case, of course, but these things do happen. Even in better quality centers, because the ratio is maxed out, teachers often work alone. In other words, visibility is crucial, but it also shouldn't be the *only* reason we choose a place.

In my child care, parents are always welcome during my open hours, and they can just show up, unannounced. They usually walk in on their own. My home is easily accessible, as well, neighbors see and hear us outside often, and both the state child care division and the USDA Food Program make surprise visits to check on things. Furthermore, I have part-time and full-time employees and substitutes, who the children know, and who constantly see how I care for the kids.

In contrast, the state and USDA typically make one *scheduled* visit to centers annually. In other words, the center knows they're coming and has the classrooms prep for the event; teachers put their sanitizers (chemical sprays for cleaning) away in a locked cupboard, they finally send any sick kids home as required by law, the room is cleaned beforehand, and the teachers follow the food program more honestly, etc. A quality home program, on the other hand, is typically *always* on top of all of those things and more. I personally want my child in a safer, more organized atmosphere.

Obviously, I'm quite biased toward small group, home-based child care programs. They're typically far better for the teachers/caregivers, better for the children, and better for the families. Especially a state certified, quality program. In fact, I'm still friends with some of the families I first began working with almost 20 years ago, and many of the other families in the time since. I can't say that for any of the children from the preschools and centers where I've taught, though. It was a far less personal experience that my in-home program provides. It's significant to me how dissimilar the two experiences and outcomes are.

I'm so passionate about quality child care, that I wrote the book **How to Start & Maintain Your Own Successful Child Care Business** for any of you interested in starting your own business. There is *always* a need for quality child care. My book is on Amazon.com in paperback and Kindle eBook formats. And it's chock full of everything I learned in my first 16 years, and everything you'll need to get going.

When it comes to placing your child in care, when it's time, you must do whatever is best for your family, of course! Along with following your gut, and checking reviews of a child care, I recommend that you look for a warm, playful atmosphere where the children are actively engaged, and fighting and chaos are limited (and supported by teachers, when it does arise, who want to help the upset children work through their feelings, to learn and grow from the experience). Look for a solid, age-appropriate curriculum, a schedule that supports all their areas of development, including both indoor and outdoor play, and including energetic play and restful play. Look for a caregiver who is health-oriented, with a low turnover rate in their staff. Look for a place that will feel like family to your children. And keep doing, at home, what you know best supports their hearts and minds!

Bishop, Jean (Lane Community College). Personal interview. 2 May 2015.

Anonymous (Oregon Research Institute). Personal interview. 2 May 2015.

Graham, Judith. "Children and Brain Development: What We Know About How Children Learn." Umaine. University of Maine, 2011. Web. 28 Apr. 2015.

Grotberg, Edith H. "A Guide to Promoting Resilience in Children: Strengthening the Human Spirit." Resilnet. Bernard Van Leer Foundation, n.d. Web. 20 Apr. 2015.

Honig, Alice Sterling. Little Kids, Big Worries: Stress-Busting Tips for Early Childhood Classrooms. Baltimore: Paul H. Brookes Publishing Co., Inc., 2010. Print.

"The Abecedarian Intervention Project." School Literacy and Culture. Rice University. N.p, n.d. Web. 20 Apr. 2015.

CHAPTER 3

Balancing Work and Family

Finding the right balance between work and family will look a little differently for everyone. Many families have two working parents, while some only have one single parent trying to keep everything functioning as smoothly as possible all on their own, while others have a working parent and a stay-at-home parent. Having a stay-at-home parent eases the burden of both parents having to work hard all day, sit in traffic, figure out dinner, get all the housework done, AND nurture the child or baby. Having a stay-at-home parent tends to put paying the bills on one parent, and cleaning, grocery shopping, cooking, and nurturing the child at home all day on the other parent. That system works very well for many families that can afford to live on only one income. Single parenting is, by far, typically the most stressful: everything falls into one parent's lap, and the child often reflects the stress of that parent. Two working parents can still mean that both of them are at work 45-50 hours per week (or even more), and spend their evenings and weekends attempting to enjoy family time while keeping up on chores and other adult obligations. No matter the parenting arrangement, finding the right swing of things relieves us all from feeling overwhelmed so we can enjoy our lives more.

I saw a quotation, recently, that read, "We only have 18 summers with our kids." What an eye-opening way of looking at how quickly our time with them flies. It may not feel that way in the thick of things -when they're three years old and throwing a tantrum in the middle of the store, or running through the house with a failed diaper and poopsplosion up their backs- but when they have grown up and moved out and become busy in their own adult lives, it can feel like it all happened in the blink of an eye. My children are turning 21 and 16, this year. I'm very thankful for having realized the importance of savoring every second of it, as soon as my first was born. We can't ever stop or rewind time, and we don't get any of it back. So, we must enjoy each moment that we can, while we can. Having a strong sense of balance and flow, senses that replace our stress, is a crucial component of that.

Balance, in part, means finding the best routine(s) for everything to run as smoothly as possible so that I may do well at work, have personal time to recharge my batteries and enjoy my own life, and give my heart to my family to keep them thriving as well as possible. I remember poignant childhood memories with my parents -I want my children's memories of me to sustain them throughout their lives, too; I remember my connection to my grandparents and want to someday leave my grandkids with the best memories and best early childhood foundation possible, as well. I nourish my family whenever I can to leave them with my best possible touch on their lives and heart, I nourish myself with "me time" (by which I mean things that bring me joy and/or peace, like trips into nature, brunch with my friends, going out for live music, taking time to meditate, making time for my Nichiren Buddhist practice, and taking time to write, etc.), so I can recharge and enjoy this life I've been given before it's over and gone, and I of course need to put my best into my work and other adult responsibilities to keep our practical needs met.

A meaningful connection to the work we do has its own benefits, beyond just keeping the bills paid, roof over our heads, and food on the table. When we find a sense of meaning and purpose in our work, it connects us to our lives and our communities in a much more profound way than what it's like when we don't find our work to be meaningful.

Loving what we do means feeling like we've found our place in the world; it means feeling like we have a lot to offer, and are needed. Having this strong sense of purpose connects us to our joy and inner authentic self far more deeply than it does to have an easy, pleasurable day and lifestyle.

Not that those things don't matter, too! Ease, relaxation, and pleasure are important facets of finding our balance. When our bodies and minds are in a state of relaxation, they can repair themselves from the damage that stress causes to our immune systems. So, down time is important. Hobbies are important. Comfort is important. Peacefulness is important. Play is important. The goal is to balance our work, our obligations, our play, and our nurturing of our families in a way that encourages us to thrive best.

Are you aware that children learn best through play? It's true. Children *learn best* by being allowed to play, explore, and create on their own terms. It's how children mimic being an adult. Really, it's how they learn to be a person like the people around them; children are sponges for learning from their environment, peers, and caregivers, and they put all of their newly found information into practice through play. They learn cause and effect through play, how to negotiate relationships with others *in* play, how to self-regulate and self-soothe when upset through play, and so much more. Interestingly, humans (mammals, in general) never outgrow the desire for play, connection, and joy. It's why so many of us have hobbies, have friends we like to do things with -for some of us, that's even just Friday night drinks at a bar after work, or even just sitting down to watch a funny show after a long day. Our play matures, as we grow, but continues to provide respite and connection no matter how old we are.

So, how do you play? I don't mean with your children. I mean what do you do for *your* play? Personally, I love jigsaw puzzles. I love word games. I love board games and card games, when I can find people to play them with me. I love going to the movie theater. I love jumping on big trampolines, and riding my bike through my neighborhood on a warm, sunny day, with the breeze in my hair. I love swimming. And I *looove* bringing out my whacky and goofy sense of humor! These are my adult forms of play.

The family that plays together, thrives together! Balance between work and play is the key. This balance looks different, too, depending on the size of your family, and the ages of your children. Younger children often require ALL of our time, as parents. Often, we have to sneak in a date night once or twice a month, with a trusted caregiver, until the child is old enough to need less constant input, supervision, discipline, and meeting of needs from us. Bigger families also have more mouths to feed, more bodies to bathe, more laundry to wash, more guidance to offer in the relationships and dynamics of the siblings, etc.

Another aspect to consider is facilitating a balance between the individuals in addition to the whole familial unit. The needs and dynamic of the whole family often differ from the needs of each individual. It's important to account for each person in the family, and still be able to feed the unit as a whole. This may mean that each child has a different extracurricular interest (or hobby, in their spare time). So, do we have all the children take turns with a favorite sport/activity each season instead of sending them all to separate events a few times per week? I'm not sure the latter allows enough down time for families and individuals. Quiet and relaxation times are hard to come by if all of our days consist of scrambling to get to school and work on time, schooling and working *all day,* heading to after school obligations, scrambling to get everyone home for a good dinner together, then homework, baths, and household clean-up all night. That's exhausting to me, just typing it out.

I'd challenge parents with a potentially tricky question: when we send our children off to a million extracurricular activities, are we doing it to get a break from parenting and engaging with them? Furthermore, are we doing it *for them,* or for us? Facing these questions may help us decide what those extra activities are worth and how they fit into the best balance for our families.

Supporting individual needs within a family may also look like respecting and incorporating everyone's favorite foods at dinner time (or leaving out the disliked ones), allowing some wiggle room within the chore assignments so that all children are learning all the tasks, but can do despised chores less often, and less-despised (liked?) chores more often, taking turns on which family game or activity to enjoy so that all people have a say, and have a turn in choosing. Respecting the family as a whole will sometimes require examining the needs of the unit over the individual. Your oldest doesn't like going to bed at 8:00 p.m., for example, but getting up early and getting everyone out the door on time runs much more smoothly if that's the bedtime for everyone. That need then takes priority over everyone having their own say.

What children don't understand, and won't, possibly into their twenties, is that we do everything *for them*. We do all that we do to provide the best lives we can offer to them. Un-thanked, for now, it's up to us to be the best role models we can be. They'll see us get knocked down or slowed down, in life, and keep going. They'll see our accomplishments, how we handle conflict resolution, how we choose to cope with stress, how we view ourselves and take care of ourselves, and how we speak to them. And they'll subconsciously repeat a lot of it in their adult years, continuing to mimic the life and people they saw in childhood as part of being grown people, now, themselves.

So, how can we give ourselves good self-care now so that we can thrive in our parenting, but also pass down good self-care practices?

- Avoid criticizing! Avoid negative talk. It cuts like a knife, unnecessarily.
- Forgive yourself, openly.
- Forgive others. It's good for *everyone* involved.
- Ask for forgiveness, as needed, openly.

- Admit mistakes and laugh about them (or cry/apologize/etc.)
- Make the time for bubble baths, face masks, and yoga, as needed.
- Take the time and energy to make healthier food choices. Start with baby steps in the right direction.
- Drink enough water throughout the day to hydrate your cells!
- Avoid caffeine after the morning, avoid drinking too late in the day (creating a full bladder at night, when you should be sleeping), and avoid eating sugar in the evening so that getting a good night's rest isn't a problem.
- What did you love to do as a child? Where can you fit those things into your life now? Can you make art with your kids, sing, write stories, play in the dirt of a family garden, explore becoming chefs together, etc.? Doing what you loved as a child connects you to your more authentic self that came into this world already knowing what it loved.
- Laugh! As often as possible.
- Work on stopping yourself when you start coming from a negative place. Channeling it more positively or humbly begins to change the way we're wired, and it teaches others to

100

eventually be brave enough to do the same.

When we're stressed, these things seem out of our reach, and even unworthy of the struggle to get there. When we purposefully figure out how we're going to create time for ourselves, though, this new function helps everything else fall into place better, and recharge our batteries better, so that we no longer have to live in that cycle of constant stress and burden. **_Stress perpetuates itself._** It never actually solves anything. It only makes itself grow, and makes it seem as if resolution isn't possible. WE have to create the resolution by changing how we've been approaching things. This is easier to do when we can unwind, back up a little bit, and start over, fresh and renewed. When we nourish ourselves, and make time to recharge our batteries and keep our flow running smoothly, we have so much more to give!

To share my own story with you, I became a single mother to my two kids when they were only 10 months and five years old. I worked long days at home to pay the bills and be the one taking care of them. They came home from school to mom, and after work, it was just the three of us having fun family time. I cooked healthy dinners, often made homemade desserts, then we played games, and talked about our day. My weekends were also devoted to them. If they went to the park, I went, too. They played with Legos together on our Saturday mornings, while I had my coffee wake up time. We rode bikes or walked together as a family to the theater for a movie. And so on. I eventually began paying a babysitter to come over while they slept on Saturday nights so I could go out dancing with friends, a few times per month. I needed that time to myself so badly! This is to say that there *are* ways we can all find time for ourselves. I've got a few suggestions:

- Have a fun date night *at least* once or twice per month! Your marriage needs evenings where you can rekindle your intimacy, just the two of you, out of parent mode. Or, if you're single, your love life deserves some attention!
- If you can't afford a babysitter/nanny, set up a trade with a trustworthy family who is looking for something similar -or some other kind of trade. Maybe you know a nanny who needs a service you can offer like housekeeping or preparing taxes?
- If you do a child care trade with another family, it can be an event that's very fun for your children: on your night(s) with all of the kids, turn it into a sleepover with games, balloons, fun snacks, and late-night movies! We remember these fun things, and the time and effort that our parents took to play with us, for the rest of our lives.
- Trade with your spouse once per month. They get one Saturday night -or morning?- free of children to catch up with their friends or hobbies, and so do you. Maybe they really miss playing guitar with their group of musician buddies, and maybe you miss catching up with your friends over brunch

and a pedicure, or what-have-you. (This is, of course, assuming that both parents are already present and attentive with their children and other adult responsibilities; if one parent already spends a lot of time away from the family to enjoy their own alone time, different priorities and boundaries should be arranged. Excessive personal time away from the family is also very out of balance, and it hurts the other family members.)

- Depending on your child's age, can *they* trade time with you? As in, if they let you meditate, undistracted, for one hour, they can have one hour of video game time, or you'll take them to the arcade for an hour, etc.

When we come from a place of being well-nurtured, instead of stressed and stretched thin, we have a far better chance of creating a lifelong friendship with our children. Although a healthy parent-child relationship comes first, a great relationship of friendship, trust, respect, and support can (and, I'd argue, *should*) be built within it. Children benefit from the closeness and kindness that a friendship brings. They grow up, this way, with friendships that never move away, never stole their first crush, nor broke their toys on purpose, etc. They grow up understanding friendship with the people who hold their closest ties, and they are then able to pass this on to their own children and grandchildren.

What are your closest friendships like? Do they offer trust, comfort, support, and joy? What a gift to include these qualities of friendship in our relationships with our children.

Trust, bonding, and play are how we reach children on their deepest levels. They're how we help them build strong self-esteem and self-trust, as well. Time spent connecting with children on *their* levels, through these things, is how we show them they matter to us, they deserve us, they can trust us, and that they are trustworthy and valuable themselves. In this, is built a friendship. When we can joke together, laugh together, intentionally respect each other's boundaries and needs, communicate openly and kindly, trust the other with our fears and vulnerabilities, enjoy creating together, and rely on each other, we have created a beautiful friendship.

Families, after all, thrive best when we leave our emotional baggage outside. When we don't leave it outside, our children adopt it. They develop an inner voice that matches our critical/painful voices towards them, they adopt our insecurities, and quirks, and they assume their worth is only what we make it out to be, by how we talk to them and treat them. When we are self-aware enough to stop ourselves from letting children push our buttons, or from provoking a power struggle between us when they long to understand their own power and therefore attempt to test us, we show them how to be people more kindly and confidently. This holds them to a higher standard for their own maturing. *Parents* must set this example, and pave the way for our babies to follow. Even in harder times, when life's challenges that arise have us feeling alone and disconnected, or overwhelmed.

At all times possible, I recommend that parents use family dinner time to really get the most out of their busy day together, and reconnect with each other. After a long day of work and school, all family members (as is developmentally-appropriate for each person, of course) can help with making dinner: one can rinse lettuce and put it in a bowl, one can boil pasta and chop veggies for the salad, and another can prepare and bake some chicken breasts (or make a quick lentil soup for vegetarian protein). One can set the table, while the other gives the dog her dinner, while another sets up her post-dinner homework that she'll be working on.

When we all come together for just half an hour (or more), it's family bonding time to unwind, settle in, nourish our bodies, enjoy something tasty, reconnect with each other by showing interest in our people's days, and sharing with them the highlights of our own, and bring up any light-hearted family matters that are in need of a good conversation. Positive "family meetings" over dinner are a great time to talk about the plans for the evening, plans for the next day, a relative coming to visit, a weekend event coming up, etc. Talking over a good meal is a great way to all get on the same page together.

I asked my friend, and local Registered Dietician, in Eugene Oregon, for her input on why families should have a sit-down dinner together every night possible. This was her thoughtful reply:

> "In our hectic world, it is essential to carve out dedicated family time together. There are

so many distractions that can keep us moving in different directions. The truth is, we spend more time apart than together, especially during the weekdays. Creating a sacred space around mealtime allows us to connect to each other and our food more deeply. In our family of 4, we have a goal to eat dinner at the table together every night. Though this is not possible all the time, we do it often enough that the pattern is well-established in our lives. We turn off all devices before we sit down, then we take turns offering gratitude for the nourishing meal we are about to consume. Slowing down to truly savor this time together allows us to connect to the many factors that converge to grace our table with abundance. We take time to appreciate the farmers who grew our food, the elements that nourished the plants (sunlight, rain, soil), and the people who prepared the meal for us (usually me!). We talk about how the food we eat literally creates and sustains every cell in our bodies. It is a profound realization that we all feel to varying degrees depending on the day. There are ways to ensure that our children are even more deeply connected to the source of their daily sustenance. Growing a garden is my favorite way to do this. Our son recently harvested an artichoke he had watched in our backyard for months. The joy I observed in him during the cutting of the stalk, preparation and then consumption of this vegetable was palpable. Our whole family experienced greater reverence for this vegetable, since we were keenly aware of where it originated, and participated in the process of nurturing its growth. If possible, encourage the kids be involved in the planning of a garden, even giving them their own little plot to design. Let them plant and water the sprouts, and observe them as they grow and change. When those vegetables are harvested, the kids will be feeling their connection to them long before they are even prepared or consumed. The next best thing to growing yourself is to visit your local farmer's market. I always ask the kids to pick out the vegetables that call to them with their bright colors and beautiful shapes. They are generally excited to eat fresh vegetables and fruits they have picked out themselves. Foods grown sustainably in our local area and picked when they are fully ripe have the highest level of nutrients possible, and the best flavor. We are signed up to receive a CSA (Community Supported Agriculture) box from a local organic farm for 22 weeks this year. We pay ahead of time to help support the farmers who are growing food for us, then are surprised by the vegetables we receive each week. We seek out creative ways to prepare them with our staple foods from home (grains, legumes, etc.). I encourage my kids to help out in the kitchen as much as possible, but I don't want to force them. I find joy in preparing foods, and I infuse love into every meal I make. I ask them to bring a positive attitude into the kitchen if they are willing to help. My son is so proud when I announce to our family that he chopped all the vegetables for our soup that night. My daughter isn't as keen on helping me cook, but if there is a baking project, she is almost always willing to assist! I find that asking them to meet me in the kitchen where their natural curiosity and interest align will bring the most fruitful experience to them, and entice them to practice their skills again and again.

Once we have the meal prepared, we try to appreciate all the colors and aromas of our food before we eat it. Bringing mindful awareness to our meal helps us to enjoy it more fully, and to really take it all in. When our bodies are relaxed, we are able to digest our foods more fully and assimilate the nutrients optimally. We are also more tuned in to our bodies' natural cues of hunger and satiety, so we tend to eat the amount of food our bodies actually need, which helps our kids grown into their bodies in a healthy way. My husband and I provide the nourishing meal at the time we would like to bring our family together (ideally around the same time every night, but this varies according to the changing nature of our busy lives!), we create the most relaxing environment possible, and then we trust our kids to eat the food their bodies are hungry for, and to eat the right

amount for them. We don't force our kids to
eat foods they don't like, but we do ask them
to take a "thank you bite" as a sign of respect
and gratitude for the food itself and the
person who has prepared it for them. If they
don't like it, they may pass on eating the rest.
We do not prepare separate meals based on
their personal likes and dislikes, but they are
each allowed one or two "no thank you"
foods, designated ahead of time. Otherwise,
we add all foods in to the rotation and they
will at least have a thank you bite each time.
It can take up to 15 times of being exposed to
a new food before a child will accept it into
their diet, so just be patient and keep trying
without adding guilt or shame to the equation
if possible. Over time, your kids will have a
varied, nutritious diet full of fruits, vegetables,
whole grains, legumes and other nourishing
whole foods you offer them. One of the
most important aspects of keeping kids
healthy with respect to their diet is to keep it
FUN!!! Add enjoyment to the experience
whenever possible. Eat with your fingers for
a meal. Cut veggies and fruits into fun
shapes. Freeze berries into ice cubes to serve
in homemade honey lemonade. Possibilities
are endless! Celebrating with food and family
is a beautiful way to express reverence for life
itself." (Jennifer Chastain, MS RD LD is a
registered dietitian working with veterans in
their homes. She is passionate about holistic
health and using food as medicine. She lives

with her permaculture-loving husband, Jesse, and their two children, Evin (11) and Rylan (8). Jennifer and Jesse share an intense desire to live a more sustainable life, and to share the ways they care for the earth and themselves with their children and other loved ones.)

Furthermore, children miss their families all day long. Do you remember how you felt having to be away from your parents when you were little? Young children long for their parents' company and security, and older children experience the insecurities of ever-changing social scenes at school, in addition to academic challenges. Middle school ages are the hardest ages. Cognitively, the child's brain has become hyper-aware of the need to fit in, they feel more out of place than ever as they become more independent -but are no longer a child and not yet an adult- they feel insecure about most things, they can become easily prone to anxiety and depression (and suicidal thoughts) at the slightest social letdown, and puberty's hormones begin to rear their ugly heads. Coming home to a positive, family environment that cooks, eats, and bonds together after a long day away from each other, then, is how children recharge their batteries. They *need* that quality family time together.

In our spare time with them, when work is out of the way, the chores are done, we've joined them in play and in meeting them on their level, they're well fed and emotionally nurtured, and we've taken grown up time for ourselves to recharge our own batteries *and* our relationship with our spouse, let's not forget to have teaching moments with them whenever we can. Chances are, school won't teach them to sew, knit, balance a checkbook, write a monthly budget, build a good credit score (I **highly** recommend a book by Suze Orman, *The Money Book for the Young, Fabulous & Broke,* for you and your older children) - money is power, in this world, and your children *deserve to understand it* so they may live empowered lives, fix a flat tire, get the dishes clean, grow food in a garden, have good handwriting, take care of our bodies, wash a dog, patch up a piece of broken furniture, mow a lawn, nor *learn to be resourceful in general.* We must give them that.

What gifts we will leave them! What gifts we will enjoy in our time with them. By finding the right routines for our busy lives, so that we may enjoy a sense of flow, and by giving as much love and care to ourselves as we do to our work, home, and children, so we can recharge instead of over-stressing, we then find the way to balance these major components of our lives. We find a way to feed all of them, and ourselves. When things develop a smoother rhythm, that rhythm tends to perpetuate itself. Life gets easier and smoother, our children reflect that relief, and our bonds are strengthened by this more enjoyable life in which we all now get to participate. In other words:

> 1. Make time to recharge your own batteries. As often as possible. Everything in life is easier and more enjoyable when our physical and emotional gas tanks are running on full instead of empty.

2. Adjust your routines to create the best flow and rhythm in your day, so you all can get out of stress mode and into a system that works instead.

3. Make trades with others for personal time, *and* to create other areas of support in your life! A trade to support better routines may mean that a neighbor drives your kids (and theirs) to school in the morning, and then you pick them all up after school, so the burden of one trip is off your hands, freeing up more time in your day. Maybe another neighbor helps you with your weekly household chores because you and your kids help her on the weekend with her gardening, or dog-sitting, etc. Or maybe he makes enough lasagna for your family (and his) on Tuesday nights, so you don't have to cook, and you in turn make enough minestrone soup on Wednesday nights so his family doesn't have to cook that night.

4. People are social animals by design: we *need* other people. We've become separated, "independent," and afraid of connecting, but it's worth it to push through that to the other side and create valuable relationships (with other trustworthy people), community, and support for each other.

5. Use family dinner time at the end of a long day to reconnect, unwind, and bond with your children and spouse. Make it a meaningful, supportive, and happy tradition they carry on to their own families.

Something commonly lacking in our lifestyles is the ability to be present in the present. Our fast-paced lives have us racing toward the future, worrying about being on time, worrying about paying all the upcoming bills, preoccupied with our Friday night plans, etc. Poverty does the same: we cannot enjoy the moment without worrying how to afford food, buy a new jacket, pay a bill, and so forth. States of stress take us away from being present in the present as well. These things distract us from enjoying what we have, where we are, who we're with, and this moment of life happening NOW that we'll never get back. Learning to slow down and stay in the present heals so much of our anxiety, stress, and disconnect. *Being present in the present moment reconnects us.*

Being present means not trying to escape what's happening in the present moment -"escaping" by doing something else, by being distracted, by becoming angry or depressed to "change the subject," by turning on the TV or smartphone to tune out the present environment- it means being attentive to our people in the present moment, really sitting (or driving, eating, playing, snuggling, etc.) attentively with them, awareness on them and awareness on ourselves instead of on some future plan/bill/stressor and the like. Present in the present moment means listening, caring, settling in to what's happening at this time, even if it's something uncomfortable. Focus like this grounds us, re-centers us, and changes our perspective. It calms the beast. It reconnects us so we may really be in our own lives, instead of ruled and driven by stress. This is how we begin to balance work and family so that everyone may thrive to their best abilities. It starts with us being willing to make a shift. Our families deserve it.

CHAPTER 4

Our Health and Wellness

I've been a food nerd for a long time. Anything food, nutrition, or health related tends to be a giant passion of mine. And I've got a long history of interest in these things, from being raised vegetarian in a holistic health-minded home, being vegan for the first four years of my twenties, having been a raw-foodist for half a year, having eaten organically for the last 20+ years, with a focus on whole foods, green veggies, a healthy pH balance, and staying well hydrated, having experimented with many dietary lifestyles like eating for my Ayurvedic dosha, for my blood type, for my genetic type, and even gluten-free (something my body didn't used to require, wheat flour now gives me hives, brain fog, and digestive issues), to now trying small amounts of fish to see how my body responds to it. I've also got a two-year degree in medicinal herbalism –with honors- and I've aced every nutrition course at my local community college. I've read and studied dozens of books on food, nutrition, and wellness in my free time, and have discussed diets and different perspectives on nutrition and wellness with countless people.

This is all to say, I consider myself having a well-rounded perspective on these things; I'm not just viewing health and wellness through one lens of experience and education, but through many. The wisdom that I have found in my 20 years of food-nerding is

1. The immense importance of eating **real** food as often as possible.
2. Recognizing the mentality and psychology behind the way many people eat: there's an identity enmeshment that often happens with our dietary choices that can be crushing to our health experience. By this, I mean that people get their egos wrapped up in how they eat, they defend how they eat as if their life depends on it, they want others to morph to that lifestyle as well, and they feel they can't separate their identities from their chosen diets. We seem to forget that food is meant to be nourishing for us on all levels, rather than disheartening, or a method of control.
3. Finding the right balance -for each of us individually- for physical, mental, and emotional health (hopefully in ways that best support environmental health, too. How we grow and raise our food can be great for Earth and humanity, or one's of its biggest detriments).

In my experience, there's an Eating Spectrum for all of us, with a lot of people living at one extreme end or the other. The first extreme is those of us with the "Life is Too Short So Eat However You Want" mentality —those of us who have never known eating well, or have given it up to eat indulgently whenever we want to, who maybe eat overly rich foods to dull our senses or cope with the world, or eat metabolism-suppressing junk foods to avoid feeling hunger (which can trigger a bunch of different emotions), who maybe eat mostly crap "food," and who have health and wellness problems because of it.

And on the other end of the spectrum, the extreme "Health Nuts" —those of us who abstain from and demonize a bunch of foods, maybe insisting that *everyone* should be eating this way without realizing that a *lot* of this country doesn't have access to (the money/affordability, the transportation needed, or even the cultural longing for) organically grown and local health foods of the purest quality, and those of us who maybe look down on others for not "eating better," ironically losing our connection to actually enjoying food, and enjoying food with others, in an attempt to eat "right." When did we go from regularly eating well and enjoying our wide array of foods, with people we cherish, to this imbalance of either not caring about quality food *or* neurotically obsessing over it?

I've known many health nuts who seem to completely over-identify with their chosen dietary habits as if they silently fear they have a certain foody reputation to uphold. Like they won't be a good enough, "pure" enough, worthy enough person who's validly living a valuable life if they don't eat rigidly and minimalistically. They tend to lecture others and even look down on them for not following the same rules of eating, in an attempt to feel better about themselves -reinforcing their beliefs- regarding their strict food choices. There's a term for this when it becomes a health condition, actually. It's called Orthorexia. Orthorexia is the obsession with denying ourselves or "purifying" ourselves through food. I hope you'll look into this term more as I won't be going into great detail on it, in this book. I feel both empathy and concern for this condition because I've lived through it. Our ego lies to us, telling us we're healthier than others who are not living the way we do. It tells us we've purified ourselves by eating like an ascetic monk. But we all deserve a more well-rounded view of how to *truly* be healthy and happy.

So, we have a multitude of people out there with really poor diets and health, and a multitude of other people wanting to use food to become their puritanical purest, but often forgetting to enjoy the process and not alienate themselves and others: *people have forgotten what it means to be somewhere, healthfully balanced, in the middle of that spectrum.* We've lost, as a society, what it means to know, be connected to, and enjoy our food. We've lost our healthy perspective on nourishment. We've lost what it means to have a balanced and loving relationship with this thing so central to our needs.

On one hand, we've got people who are so far removed from real food, they eat everything out of a box or bag, from a factory, that they found on a store shelf; we've got children who don't recognize basic vegetables and fruits because that's not how they're seeing them and eating them at home and at school;

118

we've got people binge-eating comfort foods and then hating themselves for it; we've got people feeding themselves and their children with no core understanding of what real food is and why it matters. On the other hand, we have so-called "health nuts" who shame, alienate, or look down on those who aren't health nuts in the same exact way that they are; we've got people driven to "health nuttery" out of a sense of awakening or inspiration, but with no basic understanding of whole and integral nutrition, and the importance of well-balanced meals; we've got the war of PALEO versus VEGAN eaters, and others; we've got meat-eaters who get defensive at the mere sound of the word vegetarian; we've got people attempting to perfect themselves and their identities through how they eat rather than nourishing themselves and each other.

Nourishing ourselves isn't done by food alone, after all. Nourishing ourselves means far more than just feeding our hungry bodies. Take it from someone who ate strictly incredibly nutritious, "clean" foods for years. I mean, daily veggie-packed green salads for lunch and dinner, daily pints of juiced kale and cucumber and ginger, antioxidant rich berries and soaked almonds for snacks, and no breads, dairy, sugars, caffeine, or any alcohol whatsoever. All of that radical health food wasn't enough on its own, though; *we're more than just our digestive tracts.* What I didn't understand at the time was the significance and history of food being a social bridge for us all; I thought people coming together for food was a societal weakness that ensured none of us would break the mold and start making healthier choices.

119

Predictably, I slowly-but-surely, blindly removed myself from being able to be close to anyone in my life who wasn't eating the way I was. All because I was fanatical and obsessed with trying to purify my body and self-esteem through food, rather than being in a healthy, balanced, loving relationship with food and with myself.

Don't get me wrong. I love my health nut phase and the insight it gave me into eating incredibly nutritiously. I wouldn't trade it for anything. It taught me a lot and showed me that eating well can feel really amazing. When it's done right, our bodies love it! I'm just here to say that there's so much more to eating than being rigid, fanatical, and egotistical about our food; there's so much more to living well than separating ourselves from those who are on a path of making different dietary choices for themselves.

The thing is, food isn't just nutrients; it's memories, like the way grandma's cooking smelled on Thanksgiving; it's fun and bonding with others, like eating together in the cafeteria at school or trading your trick-or-treating candy with your friends for the ones you love most; it's celebratory, of our culture's holidays, weddings, and the like; it's enriching to our friendships and families, like enjoying dinner together, teaching our children how to cook and bake their own food for themselves and for each other, gardening and enjoying our own home grown food that we worked for together, and preparing soups and hot herbal teas for our loved ones when they are ill. In this way, food is both physically *and* psychologically nourishing. If we aren't living on one extreme end of the spectrum, that is.

I think a lot of us fall into the trap of forgetting how crucial it is to support our emotional and psychological health when we are stressed. I'll give you a very personal example. When my daughter was born, she couldn't latch her mouth onto my breast properly; she couldn't swallow the milk in her mouth and hold her latch on my nipple at the same time. What this meant was that every time she swallowed a drink of milk, she lost her latch and began to suck in an extremely painful way for me. It got to the point, pretty quickly, where she was ferociously hungry every hour, I was wincing, crying, and not sleeping at all, and pretty soon I was bleeding into her mouth. Gruesome, but true.

I called my lifelong doctor, Edward Jarvis, bless his beautiful and generous soul, and asked him what to do. He told me that my baby getting my breast milk wasn't the only aspect of importance here: she and I also needed to be psychologically well together, and bonding over our feedings —not crying and dying, or so it felt. I didn't believe him —rather the *guilt* in me didn't believe him- but I felt like I had no choice (I was in pain, completely sleep-deprived, and still solely responsible for my energetic almost five year old son, our home, getting groceries and cooking, my work, and more).

Sadly, pumping milk for her had only caused me breast infections every time. So, we switched to formula and bottles. My adamant "breastfeeding only!" midwife stopped talking to me and checking in on us. A lot of militant naturalists believe breastfeeding is superior in *all* situations, a stance greatly lacking in empathy and life experience, if you

121

ask me. Guess what. At 6 months old, my daughter was STILL losing her latch on her bottles when she drank. Had it not been for my doctor's compassion and understanding of *whole health*, I would've attempted to keep breastfeeding her while my nipples were literally shredded. It was then that I started to catch a glimpse into the detriments of people and their dietary "health" snobberies. It was then that I began to glimpse the significance of letting go of my own nutritional fanaticism and opening up to a wider, broader understanding of what it means to *be well on every level.*

One of the greatest lessons I've learned in my life: food is not the enemy. How we use it as a crutch for other issues in our lives is the real problem at hand. Additionally, *how* we eat is possibly as important as what we eat! Are we eating with love? Joy? Regret? Anger? Loneliness? Peace? These things flavor our food, digestion, assimilation, and elimination, too. This isn't an argument in favor of endless chips, pizza, beer, and ice cream, by the way. That would be the other extreme of the spectrum, here. This is an argument in favor of meals that include both highly nutritious foods *and* foods that warm our hearts and souls; this is an argument in favor of food bringing people together and nourishing our sense of belonging and community; it's an argument in favor of wholeheartedly respecting the food choices of other people as they are **not** ours to make! This is an argument in favor of developing more balance and integrity.

Because diets are a privilege. They're eliminatory and they're expensive. For many people, they're hard to begin, afford, and sustain. And, historically, we had NEVER shunned food before its processed counterparts began overflowing every grocery store shelf (and restaurant dumpster). Historically, it has always been best for human beings to eat what grows seasonally and locally to us, eating whole foods instead of processed, and eating a variety of all of the food groups available to us. Our evolution has been based on eating like this, and our bodies are designed for it. In other words, diets are unnatural.

What's natural to humans is to eat the foods that grow naturally and locally to us: meats, animal milks and eggs, vegetables, nuts, fruits and honey, rice, lentils, and other grains and legumes. This is how the human race has survived and thrived. Those in Africa, for example, who *only* survive because of their access to cow blood, meat, and milk might gape at one's rantings about veganism. The Alaskan cultures who survive mainly on blubber would be shocked as well. Those relying on rice and potatoes might be baffled by Paleo dieting. Those still thriving on wild harvested foods (or fresh from the farm foods) might wonder why the heck we turn our food into processed things that make us obese, sick, and riddled with cavities.

Returning to our roots of eating real food, food raised and grown locally when possible, the foods our ancestors knew, *and* enjoying ourselves in the process —via potlucks and parties, homemade desserts and celebratory cakes, cultural traditions, and family feasts- is the key to returning to our friendship with food. We're meant to churn butter, pull kale from the garden, bake bread, and share in the dining on it by a warm hearth with happy friends and family, with full bellies and contented hearts. This is *true* nourishment. And it's delectable.

Working on a Healthier Relationship with Our Food

In addition to working on better friendships with our food, I'd also like to suggest that you take a good nutrition class at your local college. Or start learning more by reading some good used nutrition textbooks, if classes aren't currently an option. They can be obtained from your local library, read on campus, if necessary, purchased for your Amazon Kindle/app, or borrowed from a friend or community member. Although it may seem unnecessary to become better educated on nutrition, especially for those of us who already feel quite comfortable feeding other people the way we've always eaten, I have learned so many things, in studying nutrition, that I know aren't especially common knowledge for those of us without that interest.

Like, did you know that we need a lot of vitamin C every day? It only stays in the body for 24 hours and then needs to be replenished. Vitamin C is responsible for important functions like a healthy immune system, healthy gums, and healthy skin. Smokers and people exposed to smokers need extra vitamin C! B vitamins, as well, can be difficult to get enough of, even for meat-eaters, because of how our diets, corresponding absorption rates, and even farm soil quality have changed. When supplementing (not just important for vegans and vegetarians anymore), it's important to get *all* the B-vitamins. Focusing on just one, like B-12, can deplete the others. Eating too many egg whites without the yolks depletes these b-vitamins from our bodies, as does drinking alcohol. Not getting enough calcium in our diets (or eating too much protein which flushes out some of our calcium) causes our bodies to pull calcium from our bones to keep calcium levels in our blood regulated, eventually weakening our bones. Eating our leafy greens and low-sugar yogurt is so important to help compensate for this! Fiber is incredibly valuable for cleaning out our guts, supporting our immune systems, and even helping to prevent cancer. Please, please, PLEASE learn about how real food is medicine as soon as you can. Our babies deserve it. We all do.

As devoted parents and guides of these young hearts and minds, it's up to us to use the impact we have on our children's lives to give them the best start possible. It doesn't get much more basic than that which sustains us our whole lives: our relationship to food. As someone who has studied nutrition and holistic health for 20 years, and worked successfully with kids and their families for almost as long, here are my tips for providing a better experience of food and eating for our families, so that we can help foster healthier relationships with food, in their lives:

- Provide a variety of healthy food options every day. Even if you start with one small health food addition/change per day. Even if your children aren't yet responding well to healthier choices, keep offering them! Show your kids that this is NORMAL eating. Normalize it for them. They will eventually get curious and want to fit in with what everyone else is doing.

- Don't pressure, force, or shame your children, of course. Just give them options, and then support their choices. Eating should be a positive experience that leads to healthy and happy choices later in life.
- Eat what your children are eating so they see you setting the example and enjoying yourself.
- TALK about where our foods come from, the work that went into getting them from the garden or farm to our table, the nutritional value of foods (if needed, can you learn more together via library books or good websites?), what the vitamins, minerals, proteins, etc. in foods do for us in our bodies, what foods you like and why, how different cultures eat differently, and   anything else food related.
- SHOW children how to grow their own food, even if it starts with one potted tomato plant or front yard strawberry plant. Show them it's something anyone can do, and how to do it. What else can you explore growing together?
- ASK children what they like to eat on their favorite holidays, on weekends at home with you, at night for dinner, etc. Do they like a particular food just at grandma's house (she's the only one I'd ever eat broccoli for, when I was little). Are there foods they don't like, and why? Are any of those foods things that can

126

be cooked together, or made differently to be more enjoyable?

- Show them foods in books and videos, then play restaurant with a made-up menu and play foods.

- Pretend to feed baby dolls, stuffed animals, and dollhouse figurines. Pretend to have good manners, pretend to garden or farm for those foods, and pretend to try new things that seem yucky.

- Bake something together. Chop veggies and let the children put them in a   salad, soup, or stir-fry. *Make your children part of the food-loving process.*

- Include your older children in creating a menu with questions like, "Sara, would you rather have peanut butter at lunch time, or at snack time?" and "David, do you like grapes for breakfast better, or blueberries? What should we put on the breakfast menu?"

- Don't force kids to eat everything on their plate. Allow them to listen to their own bodies and appetites, and have some control over themselves.

- Do let them choose to have seconds of healthy foods. Like, more apples or more celery with peanut butter.

- Food should never be used as a punishment nor a reward!

- Don't shame your kids when they don't eat all of their food, or when they don't try new foods. They'll come around once they've seen a positive role model, and their other family

127

members, set a good example for long enough.

- We don't want children to end up associating their negative feelings with food and meal time! Exactly the opposite. Let's make the association as positive as   possible!
- Take the healthiest route possible with treats: purchase or make treats with better ingredients in them, give smaller portions of sugary and junk food   treats (like mini cupcakes for birthday parties, and trail mix instead of bags of candies), make air-popped popcorn from home instead of eating greasy chips, and buy -or make- real juice instead of soda, etc.
- Meal times should also convey and encourage good manners. With gentle, happy reminders about having better manners, as needed. It means a lot to be able to enjoy meal time with our people while also respecting their boundaries and senses. In my family, we don't allow feet on the table, we don't   allow any pounding, kicking, or yelling at the table (joking and happy behaviors are welcomed, however), no toys at the table, we keep our food on our plates instead of throwing it on the table or floor, and we don't play with our dishes. We avoid any electronics during meal times, too, so that we can be present and attentive to our food, our bodies, and to each other. We say please and thank you, as well.

- Lectures are not welcome at meal time! Keep the atmosphere warm and inviting. Save the bossy grown-up stuff for some other time.

- Silence is not ideal at meal time. This is a time to sit and bond with each other over good, healthy food and conversation, and laugh with each other, thus strengthening the joy we feel when eating. This is a time to talk about our day, talk about funny stories, tell jokes, ask a person how they're doing, ask what things they've liked about today, or hope will happen today, talk about our food favorites, why food is so good for us, and more! Meal time should be a fun time to talk and reconnect in a warm, positive manner.

- A lot of research has been done on the importance of "family-style dining." The research says that people of all ages, and families in their entirety, thrive better when they have a consistent routine of sitting down with everyone in their family to enjoy a good meal -homemade being 1000x better than not, of course. It's pretty important for children to have a family dinner at home. Food is one of our deepest survival instincts so it's imperative that we nourish kids' connections to healthy and happy eating, and to family-community dining, as well.

- Ask your younger children to use their memory and tell you what they ate yesterday or earlier in the day. What did they like or dislike about it? It's good for their cognitive capacities to strengthen memory recall.

- If children get bored or restless and start to bicker, step in with a cheerful distraction. Bring the bonding back into play. Sing a song, read a quick book and then talk about it, tell a riddle, talk about what family activities are going to happen this weekend, or even hold a lighthearted family meeting during the meal.
- Consider making up games that make food fun and interactive. Like, every day a different child gets to pick one of the vegetables we eat. Michael might choose carrots after Jo picks corn. It will feel empowering to them to get to pick for everyone.
- Make food flash cards and ask your children to tell you what they see. What colors are those foods? Are they better cooked or raw? How do they taste? Can you teach them the names of them in a second language?
- Create some food songs with your kids that become part of regular meals, or part of the time spent washing hands. Food should be exciting and make us feel good about our lives and the time we get to spend eating together!

Additionally, good fitness and a large amount of daily activity (compared to a sedentary lifestyle) are the keys to longevity. Growing up in good physical shape and good physical health makes staying in healthy shape far easier later in life. Conversely, growing up with health and obesity problems, in childhood, makes overcoming these issues later in life **much** harder. This is in no way meant to fat-shame anyone, though. I'm often disheartened by the people I see on social media (and the people I encounter in real life) shaming people for having more body fat than society tells us is attractive and ideal. I am both actively PRO-health and fitness, *and* PRO-honoring of our bodies as they are (and as they change)!

In defense of "being fat," by the way, it turns out that being skinnier isn't automatically healthier. Skinnier bodies can have higher levels of organ fat - the scary, potentially fatal kind- than heavier ones, skinnier bodies can lack the grounding and fortitude that heftier bodies can possess, skinnier bodies don't provide the same "safety net" of cushioning for falling back on during a major illness, skinnier bodies don't have as much weight bearing down to increase bone density, skinnier bodies can be underfed and therefore undernourished bodies, skinnier bodies can get colder faster, and many imbalances in health can arise from skinnier bodies, not just heavier bodies –I know multiple people, for example, whose so-called overweight bodies have impressively healthy cholesterol levels, compared to their slender friends. Yes, body fat has its place, and its purposes.

My own formerly slender body -the result of a lifetime of growing up very poor and hungry- won't be stereotyped like a chubby one often narrow-mindedly will be… as ugly, unhealthy, and lazy. Yet, the scarce menstrual flow I developed from eating so little led to an unhealthy condition similar to endometriosis; a condition called adenomyosis, that's extremely painful, makes it very hard for me to lose weight, causes internal hardening, enlargement, and scarring of my uterus, and that doctors say only a hysterectomy can relieve. Skinny did NOT come to my rescue there. (Side note: I have finally, after a dozen years of monthly misery, miraculously found a vitamin that relieves a **lot** of my intense menstrual pain and suffering -and this has been the case for everyone I've talked to that has a uterus and takes the vitamin daily. I will be adding a link on my website at loveembolden.weebly.com to read more about it. I do NOT sell it, personally, but want the world to know how amazing it is, and have access to it.)

This is the reality for many people: a hormonal imbalance has made us fat. And that same imbalance decreases the effects of dieting and exercising on our weight. Women (and anyone with a uterus) who have developed PCOS may *never* overcome obesity. People who've had hysterectomies, or who take birth control pills/devices to alleviate some of their hormonal suffering, will often gain a lot of weight. The hormonal changes of aging, and altered metabolism, will also cause a lot of people to have more body fat. Emotional scarring, as well, when a person develops a strong urge to protect themselves from intimacy or attention, can result in chubbier bodies; it's a common coping mechanism.

Overworking our livers (our livers have over 500 crucial jobs in our bodies), leading to a sluggish liver, is also a leading cause of hormones no longer being processed efficiently in the body -estrogens accumulate and reproductive disorders like PCOS, endometriosis, cancer, etc. develop; fats stop being broken down and eliminated, which contributes to accumulating excessive hormones and other fat-related health issues. Good liver cleanses are out there; Dr. Sandra Cabot's book on liver cleansing is fantastic! However, they can be extremely difficult to complete for a myriad reasons, like requiring enough money and time to focus on long-term natural healing, and having the emotional and social support to make big, necessary dietary changes. Addressing hormonal disturbances is a long process that requires a lot of discipline, holistic attention, and consistent self-care.

Some bodies are also *designed* to be heavier than what American culture tells us is the perfect model. Our white-centric mainstream media culture tells us to look like a white, plastic-surgeried, blonde Barbie on a yacht. What about the ethnicities with stronger and wider bone structures? Ethnicities with dispositions toward carrying more body fat? Cultures where bigger *is seen as beautiful?* Lineages that hand down genetic material encoded to make thicker bodies?

Yes, I fully understand the research behind the obesity epidemic —that obesity is causing our children to experience heart disease, and die younger than their parents would have; that communities of people who eat less live longer, and produce descendants who live longer, as well (if they also work harder, along with diet; activity is the key to longevity). My point isn't that obesity is the new black. My point is that body fat itself is not the devil. And it's extremely shallow to shame the human body for it.

To remedy our situation, we should be bringing people back to their food roots; children should grow up knowing what their vegetables are, and where they come from. School cafeterias should be well-funded to provide quality meals, and ban junk food/soda machines (schools should not be giving children unsupervised access to these things). Children should grow up gardening, at school if nowhere else. Urban farms should be supported (and funded) in cities, especially in poorer areas. Education on nutrition, cooking real and healthy foods, and the importance of nutritious family meals needs to become common again, especially for those of us who are living and growing up in poverty. Even a shift in priorities would allow organic produce and meat/dairy to be subsidized and more affordable to those of us who otherwise can't afford it. Really, it's up to *our society* to bridge the gap between us and real food, not just those of us who are living in it.

In defense of "being fat," we'll never make a healthier race of people by hyper-focusing on the sizes of our bodies. We won't live higher quality, more enriched lives by judging anyone on their appearance, or for their food choices! We aren't "better than they are" for not having fallen into their shoes, or for being on the side society programs us to believe is prettier. The loveliest approach to real health I've ever seen is found in giving ourselves unabashed, unhindered, loads of self-love. And in loving, accepting, and supporting our people for who they are, exactly as they are. It's a beautiful thing to be who you are, and love yourself, no matter what that looks like. That's where real healing and health is found. Love is always the best medicine.

So, let's lovingly teach children how to enjoy healthier foods, how to understand the importance of nutrition, how to be more active and less sedentary, how to focus on fitness as a method of self-love and self-care, and not from a place of shame. Focusing on fitness *is* giving ourselves a lot of love considering that it strengthens our muscles and bones, it increases the oxygen our cells, brain, and lungs receive, it changes the chemical output of our brains that is responsible for happiness/calm versus depression/anxiety/irritability, it helps reverse the damage that stress causes, and it helps us develop our physical skills and capabilities, and feel at home in our own bodies. How much fitness do you and your children commit to each day? If not a lot, yet, here are a few pointers to incorporate more use of your bodies for better fitness and health:

- Replace video game time that creates a lot of sitting time, with games that get you running, jumping, or dancing. Or have your children "earn" their video game time by being up and actively moving while they play. We don't *have* to sit to play. It's just what's usually most comfortable. That's bad for our bodies, though.
- Take a family walk after dinner. This can be family bonding time, it gets our bodies moving together, and it helps the digestive process before bedtime - a time when we want to be resting rather than expending a lot of energy to digest a big meal.

- What out-of-the-house weekend activities can you do together to get moving? There are trampoline parks, paintball palaces, bowling alleys, community swimming pools, local rock-climbing gyms, and even air hockey at the arcade.
- On the FREE side of things, we can run around at the playground, take our dog for a walk, run our dogs at the dog park, play frisbee or catch in the park, race on a local track, swim in a safe and local river swim spot, go for a day hike or nature walk, ride our bikes, and have a dance party!
- Talk to your children about what physical activities they enjoy at school. Can they join that sports team, join a club devoted to the activity, or start one? What are their friends into and how do they feel about those things?
- Drive less and walk more.
- Track your steps with a FitBit or another pedometer. I remember when, only a couple of years ago, a 5000 or 6000 step day for me was active. 10,000 seemed like it would always be unattainably too much work. I pushed myself just a little more each day, over time. Now, most of my days see 10k to 14k steps and it feels fantastic. Lighter days feel like a bit of a letdown because being more

active has *become normal* in my life. A big part of this change was moving more at work, and being active while I watch a movie in the evening and on weekends. I often jog in place and get some good exercise when I'm using my TV and computer, now. Where can you add more activity into your daily schedule?

In addition to these physical aspects of health and well-being, how we eat and how we move, I want to address a glaring void in our ability to achieve wellness in this country: the gap we experience, here, between western medicine and science, and older eastern modalities of medicine. There's a growing divide between people who swear by western medicine (i.e. pharmaceuticals, surgery, and the treating of individual symptoms), and those who swear by holistic forms of medicine (i.e. homeopathic remedies, herbal medicine, chiropractic care, attempting to heal through cleaner eating, fasting/juicing/cleansing, and looking at whole health to treat symptoms) instead.

I grew up in a household that revered the latter, and I learned to respect and appreciate what the former has to offer on my own. I have learned that having one and not the other is empty and incomplete. If the two sides of this same coin married each other, we'd have medicine that provides us with antibiotics when vitamins and herbs are not enough (and for some bacteria, sometimes, they are *not* enough), medicine that teaches us how to support our gut flora and gut health for stronger immune systems and more mental clarity, medicine that helps us understand the power of the foods we choose, and medicine that saves our lives with necessary surgeries. All while looking at the health and wellness of the whole person, rather than just their current symptoms.

After completing my two year course in Medicinal Herbalism, through The American College of Healthcare Sciences, in Portland Oregon, it became unmistakably clear to me that we do ourselves, and our children, a great disservice by discriminating against aspects of medicine that we don't understand. Holistic medicine *supports* our individual health, strength, and prevention of and recovery from illnesses, while western medicine offers us stronger medications that offer immediate results, immunizations against diseases that used to ravage humanity, and procedures like surgery for life-saving situations. These two areas of wellness need each other.

They both need what the other has to offer: western medicine relies on peer-reviewed studies and physical proof for results, while holistic medicine provides gentler remedies that support whole health (versus only individual symptoms) and strengthen our bodies' abilities to regain homeostasis. Holistic medicine teaches us natural methods of encouraging wellness that western medicine has somehow overlooked (though, even western medicine is now saying changing our food choices to healthier ones can reverse the onset of diabetes, protect us from cancer and heart attacks, and more. It took them long enough!). How can we have one and not the other?

The important factor, here, is finding trustworthy and quality sources of care. There are homeopathic doctors jumping on health craze bandwagons to make a profit, just like there are western doctors who will push prescription drugs on a client, before talking to them about health from a nutritional, fitness, and stress-reducing standpoint, specifically to rake in payouts from pharmaceutical company representatives. Corruption and greed are everywhere. That doesn't make either of these avenues of medicine bunk; it makes it critical that we find trusted practitioners of these healthcare avenues to help guide us in our pursuit of our best health possible.

Furthermore, the more we know, *from multiple angles,* the more empowered we are to make the best choices possible for our families! Having a well-rounded viewpoint on something isn't found by listening to a multitude of people who all agree with each other. Having the clearest view of something, from all angles, requires understanding it from all different sides. What do the people and experts in favor of it say? What do the people and experts against it say? What does history show us its impact has been? What *kind* of people are for or against it? How are they biased and why? Who else has a different opinion than the ones you've seen so far, and why? What does the rest of the world think, and what has its worldly history resulted in?

For example, it's impossible to miss the explosive vaccine controversy that has erupted in the media over the last few years; as more and more families have chosen to bypass routine immunizations, scientific communities and concerned families have responded with quite a backlash. Many parents who choose not to vaccinate their children, as I once did with my son and daughter, however, aren't necessarily negligent, lazy, or intentionally selfish, as many concerned pro-vaccine "pro-vaxxers" might argue or imply. I've known the distress first hand that comes with not wanting to inject who-knows-what chemicals into my brand-new baby's body. In fact, having grown up in the home of my naturalist, vegetarian, health-food-store-shopping mom, who opposed vaccines, is what had me questioning the choice for my own children 21 years ago. For me, adhering to a schedule of chemical injections for my baby wasn't a natural occurrence. So, I did some research.

In the summer of 1998, I gratefully accepted the overwhelming conclusion of all that I had read: as a healthy family not living in extreme poverty or filth, and not leaving the country any time soon, we could forego our shots thanks to herd immunity. Herd immunity is a term coined in the 70s that refers to the protection offered to the community by those who have had their vaccines. In other words, when most of a community receives its shots, the immunized members offer a kind of safety buffer to those who can't or won't get their shots (think infants who are too young, AIDS patients, cancer patients, and the rare few who are either allergic to vaccinations or unaffected by them). I was thrilled by my research excusing me from injecting my babies! I'd had too many fears about the possible consequences from shots and I worried that they were pushed on us, pretty forcefully, with a corporate greed agenda behind them.

I wasn't alone in my concerns, either. In "Embracing Vaccination...Lamentably Wrong!," Viera Scheibner declares that the state mandating of vaccinations was purely for profit. She writes, "It is a documented fact that the few remaining vaccine-producing drug companies lobbied the U.S. government and its agencies to mandate vaccines because without it they were not making any significant profit." She also relates some of the other common beliefs that have anti-vaccine "anti-vaxxers" so upset, including the fear that the ingredients in immunizations might harm us, that the strains within them make us sicker and make our immune systems weaker, and that our immune systems ought to develop their own resilience.

Even more frightening, Scheibner specifically believes vaccines cause Sudden Infant Death Syndrome and cancer, and she insists that, "In fact, there is no need to protect children from contracting infectious diseases of childhood. These diseases prime and mature the immune system... A well-nourished child will go through rubella, whooping cough, chicken pox, etc. with flying colors. They are not deadly diseases unless a child was vaccinated." Scheibner seems to see all vaccines as highly detrimental and obviously cares deeply for the natural development of one's immune system.

What parent doesn't care immensely for the health and well-being of their child, though? What parent doesn't have their child's best interests at heart when they decide there's a choice to be made between vaccinating and not vaccinating their babies? Anti-vaxxers fear immunizations because parents long deeply to protect our precious babies. But anti-vaxxers also oppose them, when there have been false alarms in the media left and right, because we're undereducated about them. And that's not so unreasonable. We have an overabundance of panic-inducing anti-vaccine stories on the internet, and a deficiency of experts in this field of medicine helping us see clearly, from as early on as possible, how and why vaccines matter so much

. Our society tells us it expects us to inject our children, but not *why*. We aren't generally informed that *one child dies of vaccine-preventable diseases every 20 seconds* in our world's poorest countries merely because they can't afford to receive inoculations ("Vaccine Delivery"), or that in countries where inoculation has decreased, out of a fear of potential side effects, old diseases make a nasty comeback (World Health Organization). Take these three countries, as discussed by the World Health Organization in "Six Common Misconceptions about Immunization," for example:

> -Great Britain, Sweden and Japan- cut back on the use of pertussis (whooping cough) vaccine because of fear about the vaccine. The effect was dramatic and immediate. In Great Britain, a drop in pertussis vaccination in 1974 was followed by an epidemic of more than 100,000 cases of

pertussis and 36 deaths by 1978. In Japan, around the same time, a drop in vaccination rates from 70% to 20%-40% led to a jump in pertussis from 393 cases and no deaths in 1974 to 13,000 cases and 41 deaths in 1979. In Sweden, the annual incidence rate of pertussis per 100,000 children of 0-6 years of age increased from 700 cases in 1981 to 3,200 in 1985.

We forget, in our bliss of a mostly-vaccinated country, the way diseases ran rampant through our society before we were graced with the development of vaccines. Moreover, not only are we often just not simply aware of the science and safety of vaccinations, but we are fed panic-inducing stories in the media and by our well-intentioned friends, co-workers, and other peers. Remember the scare created by Andrew Wakefield, the man who said the MMR immunization was *causing* autism in children, and causing major damage to their tummies and bowels? People still believe vaccinations can cause autism in a child, even though the study was done with only 11 children, "the original report made clear that the authors 'did not prove an association' between measles, mumps, and rubella (MMR) vaccine and a newly described syndrome of bowel disease and autism," but rather stated that more research needed to be done (Horton), and any correlation between the MMR shot and autism has been debunked over and over by numerous additional studies.

In fact, "...current research points to hereditary factors. In 2004, the Autism Speaks Foundation launched the Autism Genome Project in the hopes to find the genes associated with higher risk for the disease. It includes roughly 50 academic and research institutions that have pooled their data. ...Newer research leans towards genetics..." (Recame).

Even Scheibner's declaration that vaccines cause sudden infant death syndrome, or SIDS, is an assumption that isn't based in science. Some newborns who have died of SIDS, passed away around the same time they were scheduled to receive their infant DTP shots, but that doesn't mean the shots *caused* those deaths. Actually, "...when a number of well-controlled studies were conducted in the 1980s, in several of the studies, children who had recently received a DTP shot were less likely to get SIDS" (World Health Organization). As you can see, there's a profound difference between trusting in the results obtained by scientists versus thinking for ourselves that a vaccine is bad every time something happens to someone who's been vaccinated. One thing does not always cause the other.

Moreover, vaccines have a long history of ending major epidemics and continuing to protect us from the diseases that ravaged us pre-immunization. According to the Centers for Disease Control and Prevention in "What Would Happen If We Stopped Vaccinations?,"

"Nearly everyone in the U.S. got measles before there was a vaccine,

144

and hundreds died from it each year. Today, most doctors have never seen a case of the measles. More than 15,000 Americans died from diphtheria in 1921, before there was a vaccine. Only one case of diphtheria has been reported to the CDC since 2004. An epidemic of rubella (German measles) in 1964-65 infected 12 ½ million Americans, killed 2,000 babies, and caused 11,000 miscarriages. In 2012, 9 cases of rubella were reported to CDC."

Consider that in 1950, here in the U.S., there were 120,718 cases of pertussis and 1,118 deaths, yet only 2,063 cases and 6 deaths in 1978. Following the vaccine scare of the 1990s, wherein many families chose not to immunize, the number of cases disturbingly shot up from 2,000 cases to over 20,000 cases ("Reported Cases and Deaths..."). And we see the same thing now happening, in the United States, with measles outbreaks. Numerous anti-vaxxers insist that measles only causes a rash and fever, but is a childhood disease that is good for our immune systems to face sans immunizations. *History*, though, shows us that the measles can often lead to permanent hearing loss or worse, brain-swelling and death. It used to kill thousands annually, and the immunization is what has drastically dropped that number.

From the Center for Disease Control's website,

In 1912, measles became a nationally notifiable disease in the United States, requiring U.S. healthcare providers and laboratories to report all diagnosed cases. In the first decade of reporting, an average of 6,000 measles-related deaths were reported each year. In the decade before 1963 when a vaccine became available, nearly all children got measles by the time they were 15 years of age. It is estimated 3 to 4 million people in the United States were infected each year. Also, each year, among reported cases, an estimated 400 to 500 people died, 48,000 were hospitalized, and 1,000 suffered encephalitis (swelling of the brain) from measles … Measles was declared eliminated (absence of continuous disease transmission for greater than 12 months) from the United States in 2000. This was thanks to a highly effective vaccination program in the United States, as well as better measles control in the Americas region.

Measles had been eliminated, but the disease is making a comeback because so many parents have chosen not to vaccinate. These are *not* typically people who saw what life was like before the measles vaccine was created, or before the polio vaccine was created.

146

These are parents who haven't seen what disease epidemics look like, who believe the internet when it says the measles only results in a rash and mild discomfort, who don't understand how life-saving it is to entire communities when Merck donates free immunizations to third-world countries, and people who are more afraid of corporate greed than they are of potentially fatal diseases they're unfamiliar with because they had been eradicated for some time.

This isn't to say there have never been any injuries associated with vaccines, of course. In the 1980s, the National Vaccine Compensation Program was developed in order to investigate claims, compensate for vaccine-related injuries, and take the responsibility of compensation off the doctors and nurses providing the vaccines ("National Vaccine Injury Compensation Program"). What might be less known about this program, however, is that about 75% of the cases filed for compensation are dismissed ("Statistics Reports"), and, possibly most importantly, that most vaccine-related injuries are due to an *allergy* to the vaccine ("Vaccine Injury Table"), *not* that vaccines are causing autism, SIDS, and gastrointestinal problems.

So, while we have a very large benefit to humanity in being able to protect most people from so many of the ruinous illnesses of our past, we also have a very small amount of actual vaccine-related injuries, or side effects, if you'd rather. Personally, I'm a teacher working with infants, toddlers, and preschoolers and I've been in this field for almost 20 years. After 12 years of never having seen a vaccine reaction, one of the two year olds I worked with had a bad reaction to the flu shot. Because she had still been at the tail end of a cold, (and you aren't supposed to get the shot when sick, or if you have an allergy to eggs) a couple of days after the shot, she could no longer hold her own head up, and she had to be flown to specialists in Portland Oregon.

She became paralyzed by Guillain-Barré syndrome for the entire month of October, and spent November re-learning how to hold her head up, sit, crawl, walk, and run again. The message from the specialists to her parents was that they see a bad reaction like that to the flu shot every once in a while, especially if the patient has just been sick with something, but it's never fatal. They see *far too many children in their hospital die from the flu,* on the other hand. Between the influenza vaccine and influenza, only one of them is potentially fatal.

In addition, it's important to note a very common theme of responses from parents who are asked why they don't inoculate their children from diseases. In one assessment,

> "...some very interesting results emerged... Between 50% and 70% (depending on the particular vaccine) either had not heard of the vaccine, had not got around to it, or mistakenly thought their child was too young to have the vaccine. Around 15% to 20% either opposed immunisation or were concerned about side effects, and about 13% had medical reasons for

failing to immunise, or the vaccine
was unavailable (Donahoe)."

Clearly, many parents are ignorant to the details of when and why to immunize their children, while others are choosing to withhold these otherwise sought after, disease-preventing immunizations from their children because they believe panic-inducing stories in the media, and are otherwise uneducated about the science and safety behind this form of medicine that has spared so many of us from the epidemics of the past! In contrast, diseases still devastate communities in third world countries where they don't have the privilege of being able to afford vaccines. To be clear, that's thousands of families who would probably give an arm to have their children immunized and protected from the diseases killing people all around them.

Those of us choosing not to inoculate our children here, do so in the ignorant bliss of having no clue what it's like to live in a society riddled with disease. For those who have no choice but to go without inoculations in third world countries, and for those who cannot receive them here (due to cancer, AIDS, and allergic reactions to them, etc.), can you imagine the difference between being regularly exposed mainly to healthy people instead of mainly people who are sick or potentially will be? In a society of people more vulnerable to catching a highly contagious illness, what would we want for our children then?

In hindsight, I was 20 years old when I did my "research," and I jumped for the answers that rang true with what I had already wanted, which was to raise my child without immunizations just as my mama had raised me. Working with children and studying health and nutrition for the last 20 years, however, has shown me that most vaccinated children are not compromised by the injections in any way. Inoculated children are the reason a child with cancer can go to preschool and not come down with a life-threatening case of the measles from her peers. Inoculated nurses, and other adults, are the reason we can go to the hospital for a sprained ankle and not come home with potentially devastating *polio*. I like this safety buffer we've developed, those of us who look at the science and history of safety behind vaccines, because, personally, I don't want to know what it was like to live pre-vaccine, in the dark days of plague, smallpox, and skyrocketing infant mortality rates. And neither do my children.

Healthy Vegetable Recipes

To close this chapter, I'd like to offer you my favorite self-created recipes for easily and enjoyably incorporating more vegetables into your diet. Sometimes that's the first and best health change we can make because vegetables are so incredibly healthy for us, they start improving our health pretty quickly, they start changing our energy levels, and then becoming healthier starts to feel not so hard and not so unattainable. I hope you enjoy! Of course, feel free to explore these recipes with your children and alter them as meets your needs.

Homemade Jojos

Preheat your oven to 375°.

Cut one potato per person in half and then into wedges.

Add these to your casserole dish or baking pan.

Drizzle them in olive oil. Mix them until they're coated in olive oil.

Coat the wedges in garlic granules (coarser garlic powder), paprika, seas salt, and black pepper or cayenne pepper for spiciness.

Cook for 45 - 60 minutes (I like mine crunchier on the outside).

Potatoes are *rich* in potassium, vitamin C, and other nutrients, and -despite the panic about their carbohydrate content- are very good for us, when we aren't frying them or loading them up with butter, cheese, sour cream, bacon, etc. Baking them with a small amount of quality olive oil (and at this low-ish temperature to avoid ruining the oil) is a healthy way to enjoy this grounding, nourishing, affordable food.

Veggie Pizza / Veggie Calzone

Preheat your oven to 400°.

Roll flat and thin a package of store-bought (or homemade) pizza dough.

Sauté vegetables of your choice. I prefer kale, zucchini, onions, garlic, and tomatoes in a little olive oil and lemon juice or lemon pepper (lemon juice, vinegar, and tomato are excellent for cooking with kale [and spinach, and others] because they break down the oxalates in kale that many people can be sensitive to). Season to taste!

Line your dough with sesame seeds, shredded cheese of your choice, and basil/herbs of your choosing.

Cover the pizza in your cooked veggies.

Bake flat as a pizza, on an oiled pan, for 20 minutes.

*OR fold the top of the dough down over the top, cut the folded pizza into 4 (or more) sections, pinch the open sides closed, brush with olive oil, and bake for 20 minutes for a delicious calzone-like dinner.

Mexi-Salad

Prepare enough romaine lettuce for the amount of people eating.

On each salad, add loose black beans, corn, cilantro, diced avocado, and fresh salsa for dressing. Add lemon wedges on the side?

Crunch up a bunch of pico de gallo flavored tortilla chips on top.

This meal captures everything I love about Mexican food (minus the cheese and enchilada sauce) and can be eaten as a meal instead of a side salad. It's healthy and delicious!

Summer Salad

Prepare enough romaine or red leaf lettuce for everyone eating.

Add diced apples, green onions, cheese cubes, dried cranberries, diced avocados, and croutons. Additional quinoa, chicken, or turkey is up to you. These flavors all go really well together, are still delicious if you omit any of the ingredients, and this easy salad is so nutritious and satisfying!

Drizzle with honey mustard dressing.

Greek Salad

Prepare enough green leaf lettuce for everyone eating. Add minced basil, chopped tomatoes, fresh mozzarella cheese cubes, cucumber, and avocado. Drizzle with olive oil, lemon juice, balsamic vinegar, and a sprinkle of sea salt and black pepper. Do you want to add a few kalamata olives? Or a scoop of cooled down pasta? Red bell pepper? Quinoa?

Veggie Bake

Preheat your oven to 375°.

Chop 1 - 2 cups of these vegetables per person eating: carrots, broccoli, zucchini, onion, garlic, (red, orange, or yellow) bell pepper, and kale.

Add these to a casserole dish, with half an inch of water and a tablespoon of butter at the bottom (keep an eye on this while it's cooking to add more as needed when it evaporates).

Top with a layer of cheese, sprinkle seasonings like garlic granules, onion powder, lemon pepper, sea salt, and pepper on top, then douse with nutritional yeast.

Bake for half an hour or until the veggies are done.

Tomato Veggie Soup

Make a tomato-based broth by adding 1 - 2 cups of water per person eating to a medium or big pot, followed by 1 - 2 diced tomato per person added to the boiling water.

When your soup is down to bubbling away on medium heat or lower, add a spoon of quality olive oil or butter.

Toss in some sea salt, pepper, basil, lemon pepper, onion powder, and garlic powder. Season to your taste! Oregano? What do your taste buds like?

Now simmer your veggies: broccoli, carrots, celery, onion, garlic, bell pepper, kale.

Add loose beans of your choice and/or cooked pasta.

Veggie Stir-Fry

On medium (or medium-low for slower cooking) heat, in a teaspoon or three of quality olive oil, or toasted sesame oil, sauté carrots, broccoli, mushrooms, pea pods, bell peppers, onions, celery, and bean sprouts until well-cooked. Add soy sauce toward the end, when the veggies are cooked to your liking (the sodium will reduce moisture in the pan and in the food). I love this dish on a bed of very healthy brown rice.

Zucchinisagna

Steam 1 - 2 cups of chopped (or coin-sized rounds) zucchini per person eating.

Cover in shredded mozzarella and let melt.

Douse in marinara sauce.

Season with salt, pepper, garlic granules, etc., to your liking. Dish up and enjoy!

Dessert Apples

Cut ½ - 1 apple, per person eating, into slices.
Simmer in a pan with a small amount of water, on medium-low, adding small amounts of more water as needed. Add a teaspoon - tablespoon (depending on the number of apples for your family) of butter, a spoon of brown sugar, and a dash of cinnamon.
If you like these, add dried cranberries or raisins.
Simmer, stirring, until the apples are cooked and well coated by the brown sugar and cinnamon mix.

Here's to your health, wellness, and joyful living!

"What Would Happen If We Stopped Vaccinations?" Center for Disease Control and Prevention. CDC.gov. Web. 28 Nov. 2014.

"Reported Cases and Deaths from Vaccine Preventable Diseases, United States, 1950-2011." Center for Disease Control and Prevention. CDC.gov. Web. 28 Nov. 2014.

Donahoe, Mark. "Immunisation – Lessons from the current debate." *Vaccination? the Choice is Yours!* May 1997. Vol. 3. Issue 2. Alt Health Watch. 28 Nov. 2014.

"National Vaccine Injury Compensation Program." U.S. Department of Health and Human Services. Web. 28 Nov. 2014.

"Vaccine Injury Table." Health Resources and Services Administration. Web. 28 Nov. 2014.

"Statistics Reports." Health Resources and Services Administration. Web. 28 Nov. 2014.

Scheibner, Viera. "Embracing Vaccination...Lamentably Wrong!" *Chiropractic Journal.*
Oct.1994. Vol. 9 Issue 1, p39. 4p. Alt Health Watch. 28 Nov. 2014.

Recame, Michelle A. "The Immunization-Autism Myth Debunked." *International Journal of Childbirth Education.* Oct. 2014. Vol. 27. Issue 4. Academic Search Premier. 3 Dec. 2014.

Horton, Richard. "The Lessons of MMR." *The Lancet.* March 2004. Vol. 363. Academic Search Premier. 3 Dec. 2014.

"Six Common Misconceptions About Immunization." World Health Organization. Web. 5 Dec. 2014

"Vaccine Delivery." The Bill & Melinda Gates Foundation. Web. 5 Dec. 2014

CHAPTER 5

CHALLENGING CHILDHOOD EXPERIENCES

The concept of early childhood challenges pertains to both positive and negative life experiences. Positively challenging childhood experiences consist of activities that push our children out of their comfort zones just enough to grow, learn new skills, and develop a newly found sense of self-efficacy (the knowing that we are capable people). It consists of experiences that appropriately nudge our children into their next stage of development. This may be life experiences like helping our children balance on their bikes, until they get it on their own, working on sounding out phonetics until they grasp how to put sounds together and read on their own, or even potty-training in which children must get the hang of always "holding it" until they can make it to the toilet. These are big accomplishments that push forward a child's limits and ensure them that they're capable people.

Negatively speaking, challenging childhood experiences consist of events that are inappropriately too hard on our children, that create too much stress, or that create a trauma for the child. These experiences may look like yelling at toddlers to do something, instead of being by their side to offer our calm and supportive help with a task, expecting young children to act older, reacting with anger when they act like little kids instead, children having to go hungry, experiencing domestic discord or domestic violence, being expected to perform excessively academically, or excessively in sports, or being hurt by their adult caregivers, or by people the child relies on the adult to protect them from.

Life is a mixed bag, full of both positive and negative experiences. We learn (or fail to learn) to find our own balance as we navigate them. To keep the scales balanced, in their own lives, children need to be able to make a comeback from hardship, rather than feeling crushed or broken by it. This ability to bounce back from negative experiences is found when we cultivate a strong sense of resilience. Adults can and must help foster this in children, whenever possible, by providing guided learning opportunities appropriate to how the child is developing, and by helping to eliminate and prevent sources of unnecessary stress and negativity. As we talked about earlier on in this book, chronic stress is so toxic, it can have many long-term consequences that shorten the lifespan of the child, and decrease the quality of living within the lifespan. We clearly must give them the tools they will need to recover.

It's not just our children going through the hardest times that need a core sense of resilience, though. Our kids who are being raised in homes where everything is provided to them and life is easy may also be missing the development of this critical characteristic that they'll need later in life. Some people would view this as children who grow up with a sense of entitlement; they don't have to work for what they want and need, and they very possibly never have to struggle for it. While these children have it much easier than children living with more stressors and negative experiences, *all* kids should know the personal strength of being able to bounce back from setbacks. *All* people eventually need to have this characteristic in their back pockets.

So, let's take a look at what builds resilience. Some people are naturally born into this life with the temperament of looking out for themselves, ready to pioneer their way through life, and are never knocked down by much for long! They come into life ready to go after what they want, clear people out of the way to get it, and don't let struggles hold them back. Most of us, on the other hand, have to hone our survival instincts and the self-worth required to always forge ahead, no matter what it is we are facing. Most of us need to build the skills required to handle the harder times in life, and a reason to want to keep doing so.

We help children develop a resilient nature by facilitating opportunities for them to learn to be resourceful, and opportunities to explore just how capable they can be. We embolden the development of a resilient nature by letting children explore how to handle a perplexing situation (the adult is here to help them take their critical thinking skills to the next level, instead of doing the thinking for them), by supporting children in learning from their mistakes (without turning it into a lecture, as naturally occurring consequences tend to speak for themselves), and by helping children work for what they want, rather than effortlessly handing them everything they desire on a silver platter. The goal is to teach children how to think for themselves, how to be resourceful in the face of opposition or challenge, and how to push themselves further (safely) than they've gone before -

to expand their own knowing of their limits, and become aware that they can always go further than they'd previously thought.

Children need as many experiences (safely guided by their parents or trustworthy caregivers) of doing things on their own as possible. They need to explore what it's like to come up with solutions resourcefully. That could be deciding what to cook for the family tonight, wherein they have to choose foods for a well-balanced meal, figure out how to cook them all, learn the timing on preparing a variety of separate foods, fix any predicaments that arise (like water boiling over, or rice sticking to a pan and burning), attempt to satisfy everyone's hunger and tastes -with the pressure of their judgment riding on this task- and then clean up the preparation mess (unless the family does this for the person who has cooked, to keep the scales of job duties more even).

Alternatively, maybe they're learning how to budget their allowance and devising a plan for saving up for something they want to buy when they have enough, or how to wash a car and detail it, or how to garden and eliminate pests naturally, or how to clean out the red paint their art project got into the carpet, or they're leading the adventure on the family nature hike today, and so much more. We must let them practice trying things they haven't done before, and experience new activities that are just barely beyond what they've been responsible for before. This is how we nudge them forward in hands-on, safely guided, development of knowledge through experience.

Indeed, children thrive on being given developmentally appropriate tasks -even if they seem irritated at the time, by being given a chore. Although they often turn to more fun or relaxing measures of connecting with life around them, like playing games with friends or watching cartoons, children are born sponges, hungry and ready to "learn how to be a person" from the people around them. Adults taking our time and energy to help children learn and grow makes them feel valued and valuable. And this time and attention contributes later to a sense of capability that carries through into the rest of their lives. Children who don't receive these encouraging experiences in childhood, often grow up to feel easily defeated, to believe they don't deserve much, and to work less toward building positive experiences and a more enriching life for themselves and their own families.

This isn't to say we load children up with tasks and a checklist to complete; we don't dump our own chores onto them in the name of teaching them valuable life lessons; we don't leave children hanging to wade through a difficult situation on their own. We carry the burden of life's obligations *with* them. We walk through deciphering life's mysteries *with* them. We are right by their side taking on what life requires from us *with* them. We're here to answer their questions, pull their curiosity and receptivity into teaching moments with them, encourage long conversations, and do our best to give them their most well-rounded view of life. The more they know, the more they can grow.

I interviewed local teacher, Megan Barella and she gave some excellent answers to my questions.

Interview question: What are common negatively challenging experiences that children face? How do we best help them through this?

Megan: A part of life is struggle, and it's part of what connects us as a people. We all share a universal thread of inherent goodness - which includes our positivity, strengths, and happiness. But, we also are connected to one another by a shared experience of negativity, challenges, and stress that we can't escape from. The best thing we can do as parents is to help our children develop the inner skill set of resiliency to ride the storms of life.

Sadly, more and more children are survivors of Adverse Childhood Experiences (ACE's) and trauma, including child abuse and neglect. So even if our own children aren't trauma survivors, they will know children who are trauma survivors. Not always, but very often it's the children who have been hurt the most in life who are prone to challenging behavior, and hurting or being hurt by other children. It's important to define compassion for our children, as a concern for the sad things that happen to others, so they can understand that hurtful behavior only happens when we're hurting inside. From that place, how can we help others who are hurting and how can we be a good friend to ourselves when we are the ones hurting inside.

Aside from ACE's, all of experience daily stress and challenges during transition times. Transition times include bedtime and getting out the door to school, as

well as moving, switching grades or schools, and changes in the family dynamic. The best thing we can do for our children is to honor that challenges help us grow and become stronger as a people. By taking time to talk with our children in calm moments about life transitions, we prepare them for the life challenges they will face. We can also engage them in problem solving by the Positive Discipline tool "Curiosity Questions," or the use of "what?" or "how?" questions. A couple examples of Curiosity Questions include, "What do you think would help make the mornings easier?"
"How can we work together as a team?"

Interview question: What is the importance of resilience and how do we help them foster it?

Megan: Resiliency is everything in life! We can't control what happens to our children, but we can equip them with the skills to ride the waves of life to grow stronger in who they are through their challenges. From a young age, we can teach our children that every challenging situation has a silver lining, life lesson, or as Mr. Rogers reminds us, there are always "helpers" present with us to get us through the hard times in life.

The best way to foster resiliency in our children? Through our own modeling! Do to mirror neurons, children truly are reflecting back our thoughts and emotional states as their actually grow their developing brains off of our adult brains. How do you support yourself during stressful times and setbacks in life? Do you have an unshakable faith, belief, and trust in yourself to get you through life's challenges? The answers to these two questions speak worlds to your child's resiliency. As I jokingly tell parents in my community, "Don't worry about your kids! Focus on you." While that of course isn't totally true or even possible, by focusing on your positive personal development, and increasing your support and tools, you are directly building the same skill set in your children. That is true parenting power!

Interview question: What positively challenging experiences can we introduce into their lives to help them grow, trust in their capabilities, and recover from previous (or future) setbacks? How and why?

Megan: For a long time, we thought praise developed self-esteem. Now we know that praise just builds "approval junkies" who need validation from others in order to feel good about themselves. Please don't feel bad if you're using praise with your children! What we say in Positive Discipline is that, "Praise is like candy. A little bit is ok, but we don't want our kids to live on a solid diet of praise."

If we're not using praise, how are we developing a generation of children who trust in themselves, are resilient, and have the skills to be successful and happy in life from the inside out? Teach our children life skills! Research shows that indeed it is the teaching of life skills - not praise- that develops self-esteem in children.

As today is the most stressful time in human history to be a parent, it is very challenging to find the time, energy, and patience to teach our children how to do laundry, the dishes or yard work. Yet, it truly is developing these life skills that sets the stage for our children to be successful in life, and to gain first-hand experience with real-life setbacks. (You can find Megan's work online at www.meganbarella.com.)

Another technique to help children develop a resilient nature is by creating strong, stable, supportive relationships with them in their lives. When we are their rock and foundation, they know they aren't alone in this world, and that there's a reason to go on. When someone healthy and strong and supportive loves them, they come to *know* they are worthy of a great person's love. This, of course, is amplified when they have the solid love of a whole family. In fact, in *A Child's World: Infancy through Adolescence,* the authors say, "The two most important protective factors that help children and adolescents overcome stress and contribute to resilience are *good familial relationships* and *cognitive functioning* (p.419)." The support children feel from the members of their family and community goes a long way toward their sense of being able to face challenges and make it in this world.

Along with realizing they are capable, and knowing they are loved and needed, a resilient character is formed by having a sense of purpose and meaning in this life. For me, in my tough childhood, that was raising my little sister. It was emboldening to me, feeling that she needed me to be there for her and be good to her, but most importantly, my sense of responsibility to her gave me a deep purpose that fueled me. Children need to have things for which they're responsible. They learn they're capable through those things, they feel needed, and they develop purpose.

Sexism is a negative challenge so deeply enmeshed in our cultural programming it takes most of us many years to see outside of what we've been taught. Girls grow up seeing everywhere around them -on TV, movies, magazine pictures, websites, in personal relationships, and stories- that girls and women are measured and valued according to their beauty and pleasant demeanors, manners, and servitude. Girls are taught to be gentle and likable (instead of being leaders; instead of being assertive), be desirable without being purposefully slutty, be nurturing to everyone around us (except ourselves), and be tiny and out of the way of the (big, important) men. Women have been taught to be sidekicks who are good at looking pretty and at quietly making sandwiches for the men.

Boys, on the other hand, are taught to be tough, compartmentalize their feelings away from everyone (including themselves), "suck it up, buttercup" and "man up," to withhold nurturing ("don't be a sissy"), to attempt to be the leader in charge at all times, to be the head of the family who provides everything materialistic, to keep it all running smoothly, that their value will eventually lie in how much money they make and what their career status is, and also that their value as *a real man* lies in conquering as many women as possible, and participating in their objectification all along the way -because girls' and women's first jobs are to be gorgeous and conquerable supportive roles, remember? And "boys will be boys." ...For as long as we teach them that, anyway.

We don't see much in between these two narratives, aside from the allowance of tomboys, though there is finally becoming more and more of a safe space for gender neutral and gender fluid children and adults. We're starting to head toward being a world that allows people to fall outside of the spectrum we've been taught on how to be a woman the right way and how to be a man the right way, so that others may exist and thrive, too. Requiring girls to fit one strict mold and boys to fit the other has come at the expense of people not being able to just be who they authentically are without completely rebelling against society and alienating themselves, or worse, becoming the subject of hate crimes and bigotry for not falling within the narrow lines. This has been a detriment to humanity for far too long.

We *must* open this up by teaching our girls how to speak up for themselves, to be heard, to be big and important and powerful, too! And even just to say, "No" and "I need you to stop _____" much more often. We must teach our boys to express their feelings, fears, and vulnerabilities, to be okay with asking for help, to be nurturing and loyal to the girls who've been raised to be this way as well, and to be brave enough to help protect girls rather than objectifying them. We need to balance the scales for our children, and teach them to *be themselves, be authentically them, and be true to themselves.*

A very real, very necessary route to fixing this deeply ingrained sexism, is in changing the materials and role models that children grow up with. *Representation makes or breaks us.* We MUST see girls and women who are independently and capably able of caring for themselves, who are equals, who are strong, and who are happy this way. We MUST see boys and men with developed emotional intelligence: boys and men who are in touch with their feelings, who know how to communicate, who respect other human beings -female, male, and other- who know how to be equals and partners with girls and women, who are nurturing, receptive, and supportive, and who are brave enough to be authentically themselves.

Children's literature is one important place from which to make dramatic and long-lasting changes in the views and beliefs of our society because it can be used to subvert those same messages that have been telling children for centuries that men are meant to be powerful and women are meant merely to aspire to be lovable, acceptable, and *deemed worthy* by men. The impact here can be huge considering our sense of identity begins so very early in life and our childhood stories often shape, inspire, and nourish us in our upbringings.

The World Health Organization, and other early childhood experts, report that the human brain develops incredibly quickly in early childhood and, during that time, neural pathways either develop due to stimulation or are lost forever due to neglect. It's the first eight years of environment, and stimulation or neglect, that shape the rest of the child's life. The messages we feed our children during this time are paramount in how they come to see themselves and the world. So, while it's remarkable to work to enlighten adults who are set in the ways of their cultural programming, it's also wise to raise millions of children *enlightened from youth*.

So much attention has recently been brought to the importance of eliminating gender bias from children's stories, in fact, that in 2001, the Amelia Bloomer Project was put into effect by the American Library Association Social Responsibilities Round Table's Feminist Taskforce, creating an annual list of "quality feminist literature for youth" (Law et al 5). The project aids us, parents and teachers and librarians and so on, in attaining the very literature that helps dissolve sexism when it can be so tricky to find on our own in a vast sea of traditional written works. As described in "All About Amelia: The Amelia Bloomer Project,"

> When many books continue to present stereotypical images of women and girls, young people of all genders need to be able to find books that celebrate courageous women and girls who are portrayed not simply as "spunky" or "feisty," but as brave, confident females actively shaping their own destinies and breaking barriers to defy stereotypes and societal limitations. Girls need books that will help them to recognize, understand, and resist systemic sexism around them, to claim their voices, and to be self-possessed. These books also encourage girls and

young women to overcome issues body image and to love themselves for whom they really are, in defiance of the mainstream media's ongoing obsession with glamour, weight loss, and conventional appearance. In the process, new cultural contexts are created, honoring the diversity, validity, and beauty of all girls and women (Law et al 4).

Possibly following in the footsteps of the Amelia Bloomer Project, there are great suggested reading lists on Amazon.com, put together by consumers, on "children's books with a feminist message." The variety in content is growing. However, at the time of writing this book, most of the children's books on these lists are of white children. People of Color are often under-represented in day-to-day media, or are represented in ways that fortify the stereotypes we've been taught. It's way past time to fix that. Thankfully, more and more parents are paying attention to the stories that fill and guide their children's minds.

Others argue against changing the structure and style of traditional children's stories and fairy tales. For example, as *Time* magazine published in "Feminist Folk and Fairy Tales," from as far back as 1981, Psychologist Bruno Bettelheim thinks traditional fairy tales are important as they are because, "beauty or handsomeness is a routine signal to the child of moral worth. Marrying and living happily ever after tells children that they are worthy of love and can find it when the time comes" and that children identify with the weak character rather than the strong one and need to make sense of the world through that identification.

However, these are typical justifications of worn out practices, seen through the traditional anti-egalitarian goggles of our sexist society. They're based from a viewpoint that is puppeteered by those thriving on our system of white male privilege. It's long past time to see outside of that confine, but there can be no change in vision if we don't remove our blinders! In other words, it won't be the poster children of a sexist society telling us how to dissolve our sexist society. Fortunately, we have authors who see outside the box, who are breaking the rules, breaking the mold, and producing children's stories in which, hold onto your hats, *the females are also empowered.*

One story which not only empowers the leading female character, but also shows us how ridiculous it seems when one sex is deemed more powerful and respectable than another, is Mary Pope Osborne's *The Brave Little Seamstress*, illustrated by Giselle Potter. The lead character is a young seamstress who, on a journey, becomes mistaken for a warrior-woman. The seamstress is quick-thinking and courageous and comes to experience a great adventure of tricking giants, taming a unicorn, and catching a wild boar for a king who then betrays her. One of his knights who had grown to appreciate the spirit of the seamstress warned her. She then devised a plan that sent the king and his knights running and screaming from her. She went on to propose to her knight, who joyfully accepted, and ruled over the land as everyone's beloved Queen for the rest of her long, wonderful life. She was so loved and admired that her story became a legend that many people often sang about:

> Out of a seamstress
> A great queen was made,
> As kind and wise
> As she was strong and brave.

Attempting to balance the scales in a much subtler way, we have another book of Osborne's, titled *Kate and the Beanstalk*, also illustrated by Potter. This story takes the traditional tale of *Jack and the Beanstalk* and provides us with female characters instead. Here, Kate bravely conquers the mean, nasty giant (with indirect help from the giant's kitchen-bound wife) and returns her mother to their rightful castle. Surprise! The castle really belongs to Kate and her mother, her fairy godmother gave her those magical beans, and the conquered giant's lovely wife gets to stay on cooking for them.

Although *Kate and the Beanstalk* could have done more to break through the typical barriers of traditional children's stories, the changes it did make are a step in the right direction toward empowering girls and women. I especially like the part where Kate was asked if she was afraid to right the wrongs of the mean, nasty giant and she responded, "I don't think so. I fear nothing when I'm doing right. How can I help?" More than just the typical "be a good girl who everyone likes" message, this moral tells girls that they can right the world when they bravely follow what they feel is right. It tells them to listen to their hearts and instincts, to trust themselves, and to allow that trust to fuel their bravery. Imagine a world in which girls are taught they're safe to follow their own paths and define who they are on their own. Imagine a world in which women believe in themselves. Now, there's a story worth writing.

A common result of learning to cope with life's stressors, as we get older, is both the internalizing of feelings: expressed as anxiety, depression, and fearfulness, or externalized feelings: expressed as anger, defensiveness, and violence. Angry children tend to rebel, seeking an independent sense of renewed power that is theirs and theirs alone; their anger may be covering the root feeling of grief - the grief of having felt their power taken away from them at some point, or often, in their upbringing. Angry children need healthy outlets for their energy, to talk through their feelings, space to breathe into these feelings and get in touch with their roots, and develop better ways of expressing their need for power and independence in life.

Anxious children tend to self-harm, when life feels like too much, seeking a way to bring themselves back into their bodies when their overwhelmed senses have caused their minds to detach and try to "turn off," for a bit of a break. Anxiety and depression, amongst our children and teens, has become so prevalent, recently, that Time Magazine ran an article about the epidemic of it in this country. More and

173

more of our youth are finding themselves feeling paralyzed by their fear of what life throws at them, defeated by depression and feelings of worthlessness, and even suicidal. Experts have also found that anxiety and depression often go hand in hand. Where there is one, there is usually the other.

When we've been taken over by anxiety and depression, we've lost our sense of being powerful in our own lives. We've lost the feeling of being in charge of ourselves and our outcomes. A feeling of helplessness has taken over, and is now behind the wheel and driving us. In some cases, such as major chemical imbalances in the brain, or after the survival of extreme trauma to oneself, psychiatric treatment and medication may be the only things that bring any relief. In other cases, though, we can look to naturally supportive substances and techniques. Really, no one can pull someone out of depression and anxiety except for the individual experiencing these things. We *can* be here accepting their feelings, listening to their needs and boundaries, offering our support and companionship, and never giving up on them. We can also be aware of a few things that tend to help basic anxiety and depression most:

- Allowing a person to face and work through their own feelings.
- Supportive of feelings when I'm facing my own pain, I'm fond of talking to the piece of our inner child that was hurt (or adult self, if trauma happened later in life), and reassuring them that we still love them, life is safer now, we still want them here, and they deserved

174

better than to have been so hurt. Can your child talk to her/his/their hurt self, thus aiming self-love into this shadow area?

- A healthy diet that provides enough quality sources of the B-vitamins, vitamin D, calcium, magnesium, and potassium, hydration via plenty of clean water (this supports our energy levels and cellular elimination of waste), and daily vegetables, soluble fiber, and probiotics for gut health.

- Daily exercise that gets the heart pumping helps regulate and support the mood chemicals our brains produce.

- Certain herbs fight anxiety and depression, enhancing well-being. Look more into the safe and effective use of Saint John's Wort tea, or topical salve, and Milky Oats Tops Tincture: This remedy has excellent medicinal value for the entire nervous system. It is nourishing, calming, and stabilizing to the brain, spinal column, and nerves. It very gently elevates one's mood and is therefore beneficial to those suffering with mild to moderate depression.

- Meditation! Meditation is calming to the mind, calming to our pain bodies that are off the hook when we're experiencing anxiety and/or depression, and calming to our physical bodies and nervous systems that need to *relax* to recover from heightened states of stress and negative emotions.

Meditation is a technique that can look very different, depending on the kind you practice. Some people sit quietly with calming or inspirational instrumental music on in the background, paying attention to the breath they inhale and the breath they exhale, attempting to quiet the mind. Others may sit quietly and send light and love to their internal organs, giving gratitude to their bodies. Others may focus, eyes closed, on the area behind the "third eye" portion of the forehead, while they slow their breathing and silently repeat a mantra in their minds, like, "Om Mani Padme Hum" or "I am at peace now. I am love, I am light, I am peace"

Children can and should be taught such a powerful way to sit with ourselves, quiet ourselves, and notice the thoughts and feelings that come up for us when we let ourselves take a moment for relaxation, self-awareness, and a calming of our energies. I picked up the interest from my mom, when I was only about nine years old, and went on as a teenager (through my adult years) to experiment with Sanskrit chanting, kundalini yoga, visualizations, chakra work, and eventually Reiki, shamanic journeying and retrievals, and my current religion, Nichiren Buddhism and our Buddhist chanting. These practices have greatly healed my old traumas and changed the way I respond to the world.

With enough practice, meditation eventually becomes a very grounding method for coming back to ourselves, letting go of the upsetting emotions trying to drive behind our wheel, and even releasing old traumas. It's excellent at reducing our stress levels, and helping us to recharge our batteries. I highly recommend exploring different types of meditation, until you find the one that inspires you, and then model it for your children, and create a practice with them that they can enjoy. What fits into their schedule and routines better, 5 minutes or 30? That will be up to your family to determine. Maybe it begins as a Saturday morning family event, and then blossoms into a nightly pre-bedtime activity. It's worth giving a chance to discover the benefits for yourself!

"Feminist Folk and Fairy Tales." *Time* 20 July 1981: 64. *Academic Search Premier*. Web. 31 July 2013.

Law, Jennie S., McCoy, Maureen., Olshewsky, Beth., Semifero, Angela. *Young Adult Library Services*. Spring 2012: 4-6. *Academic Search Premier*. Web. 31 July 2013.

Martorell Gabriela., Papalia, Diane E., Duskin Feldman, Ruth., *A Child's World: Infancy through Adolescence, 13th Edition*. New York. McGraw-Hill Education, 2014. Print.

Osborne, Mary Pope. *The Brave Little Seamstress*. New York. Atheneum Books for Young Readers, 2002. Print.

Osborne, Mary Pope. *Kate and the Beanstalk*. New York. Atheneum Books for Young Readers, 2000. Print.

"World Health Organization Fact Sheet #332: Early Child Development." *WHO*. Aug. 2009. Web. 31 July 20

CHAPTER 6

The Things Children Have Taught Me

What do you need right now? Children have taught me that this question is like pure gold. When children are upset, it's because they feel their needs haven't been met. This doesn't change much, as we age and mature. Throughout our lives, our most fundamental needs tend to stay the same: we must eat, we must sleep and relax, we must protect our bodies from extreme temperatures and illnesses, and we need to feel loved. We long to feel heard and valued, rather than alone. It insures us we have a place and a purpose. Young children will find ways of letting their caregiver know they're hungry, before they can speak: crying, tugging on their high chair, pointing at food, etc. It's the job of the parent to learn to decipher these cues. Eventually, we learn to say, "I'm hungry," and to secure our own food. We learn to say, "I need to get some sleep," or "I don't feel good. I need rest and medicine."

Emotional feelings and needs, on the other hand, are tricky. So many of us never really learn how to interpret our inner emotional storms, let alone articulate them, let alone stay grounded while they occur, let alone go straight to asking for what we need. People are often caught up in the whirlwind of their feelings and, no matter our ages -this doesn't seem to be something we outgrow- they need their loved ones to be the calm in the eye of the storm. Loved ones must remember to see into the heart of things when their person or child is upset by determining:

1. What's the root feeling they feel underneath their storm, and why?
2. Which of their needs feels unmet to cause this storm?
3. How can I help them get their needs met?
4. ASK, "What do you need right now?"

This is how we join people in getting their needs met, in bridging the gap that feels wider when we're upset, and in going to the heart of matters with people. Children have taught me that if they can - often helplessly- put their needs out there, trusting others to assist them, we can, too. If they can open their hearts to new friends, in the face of stress, under

182

the weight of change, in the midst of a fast-paced society, to big feelings and the risk of trusting others... we can, too. Sometimes that begins with forgiving ourselves. For the criticisms, judgments, and imperfections we hold against ourselves. For the way others "made" us feel before. For the embarrassments, flaws, and mistakes of our past. When we have forgiven, these things no longer have a hold over us, and we can finally move forward. Forgiveness, and openness to connecting and creating together, saves us all.

Forgiveness is so incredibly significant, that I wrote this piece for my book (available in paperback and Kindle eBook on Amazon) *A Movement of Courage: Connecting More Deeply for a Happier Life:*

> Forgiveness is the root of compassion... Forgiveness is the gift that reminds us we're all equal. We're all in this together, struggling and
>
> coping and trying to make our way through it all. We're all laughing and loving and living, and grieving and dying. We're all doing the best that we can with what we have at the time. Forgiveness accepts that reality. Forgiveness heals our pain toward another person because it is humble, it's wiser than our pain, and because forgiveness is peace. When we forgive a person for being human, when we forgive ourselves for our negative reactions to them, we open our hearts back up so that compassion may flow again, and nourish us again. Forgiveness toward *ourselves*

is a crucial part of creating self-love. It heals the voice that tells us to be ashamed of who we are, that tells us we're not good enough, in some or many ways.... It's how we shine instead of shadow... Our light shines brighter the deeper we connect, and the deeper we connect the more our lights can shine. So, connecting more deeply is also at the heart of our happiness. When I say this, I mean connecting to others, but also connecting to ourselves, connecting to the lives we are experiencing, and connecting to happiness and fulfillment. This begins to happen for us as we practice living from the heart, personal integrity, and forgiveness and compassion.

Being good to children, just as adults *should have been good to us,* when we were little, means breaking the chains of the negative parenting we were given. It's not always just parents, of course. It's the alcoholic uncle, or dad's sneaky friend. It's the babysitter or teacher that was mean to you when no one else was looking. It's the grandparent or neighbor you were terrified of. Or even just the mean older kids down the road. I remember clearly the people who were unfriendly and belittling with me. The people who showed me respect and joy saved my life from those negative influences. So, how can we be that to the children in our lives?

We have a tendency, as people, to follow in the footsteps of our childhood role models. Often blindly. We subconsciously mirror what we were shown, until we grow so much that we can finally see from outside our bubble, and begin to pave our own way. Until then, we tend to repeat what we were given because it's how we were taught to be adults. This goes layers and layers and layers deep for us. As a brave and conscientious parent, what steps will you need to take to end those kinds of cycles in your life, now?

Having come to the end of this book, I hope you'll take a moment to use this couple of pages of workbook space as a journal entry to reflect on the qualities and dynamics you'd like to improve upon in your interactions with your children. Then come back in a few months to see what has changed and what hasn't.

What are your parenting style and attachment style? And how would you like to change how you express these qualities?

_____

_____

_____

_____

What are your children's temperament types and attachment styles? How do they best get their needs met? How can you best support them and guide them, knowing this?

_____

_____

_____

_____

_____

_____

What are your spouse's parenting style and attachment style? How could they change how they express these qualities to better support the children/family, while still having their own needs met?

_____

_____

_____

_____

_____

How have your most positive childhood influences impacted you?

_____

_____

_____

_____

_____

_____

How have your negative childhood influences
impacted you?

_____

_____

_____

How have you already broken the cycle of these
negative influences to give your kiddos better?

_____

_____

_____

_____

How can you further break the cycle of these negative influences?

_____

_____

_____

_____

_____

What kind of person was the adult you needed, when you were a kid? If you're going to be/become that kind of adult for the children in your life, what does s/he look like, sound like, laugh like, support like, forgive like, etc.?

_____

_____

_____

_____

New activities and routines you'd like to incorporate into your daily lives, and why:

_____

_____

_____

_____

_____

What are your new goals for yourself and for your family? What needs to happen to support these coming to fruition?

_____

_____

_____

_____

_____

Our child-sponges will take our best and our worst, no matter what we *intend* to show them, and, mirroring them back to us, will adopt those characteristics as their own. They only sometimes hear our words, but they *always* pick up on our fears, our values, our quirks, our reactions, our voices, our mannerisms, our baggage, our interests, and our joys. Not much gets by them. We teach them so much, and pass on so much, just by being who we are. Self-awareness is crucial for making sure we're being our own personal best, in this process. Honesty, humility, and self-forgiveness also help us pave the best and truest path with them. We touch their lives with these qualities when we are brave enough and kind enough to display them. Trying to be right all the time, instead, is just the ego speaking (and very possibly the voices of our own childhood caregivers) -it makes us stuck in defensiveness instead of open to growth.

In my many years of working closely with children, life has taught me this about them: they are beautiful examples of what it means to be true to who you are, connected to your life, connected to the present moment, and openly vulnerable, pure-hearted, giving, and forgiving beings. So many of us outgrow these qualities, as we grow up in a world that regularly showers us with frustrations, betrayals, obligations, setbacks, and heartbreak. Our hearts become closed off and our spirits become weary. Then we wonder, as adults, where we went wrong and what's missing in our lives. Children can show us the way back to ourselves, if we're listening and paying attention.

In fact, from what I've seen, children -just by being children- bring us face to face with our own childhood feelings, our inner child, and our "demons" from long ago. This results in adults who love and value children, but also in adults who fear and are uncomfortable around kids, instead. We can heal that hurt and awkward dimension of ourselves, though, if we're open to children, and receptive to healing. Spending quality time with children can re-mind us that it's okay to be who we authentically are; it's safe to be vulnerable and honest with the expression of ourselves, even when we fear rejection; it's healthy to slow down and bring our attention into enjoying the moment; it's brave to come from a place of love rather than our default negative feelings of fear and irritation.

Being kind to children is where we begin; their goodness will guide us the rest of the way. It's our job to be courageously honest with ourselves about our feelings that arise when we're with them. If we've had a hard upbringing, it's especially important for us be good to the children who enter our lives, just as the adults in our childhood should have been good to us. Giving to children the kindness that should've been given to us helps us heal our wounded inner child. We also break the chains of negativity and abuse that were handed down to us in our youth. We break the generational cycle of continuing to force outdated methods of raising children upon them, when we redesign the mold from which we're parenting. Children can give us this gift, and in return, we can become adults who live and love more authentically, therein setting examples for other children to do the same. We need them as much as they need us.

This initially requires the courage to commit to more self-awareness and reflection. What can we learn from the people who hurt us or put us down when we were kids and teenagers? What feelings, responses, and characteristics did this kind of treatment build in us? What can we learn about the pain *THEY* lived with, the pain that was so strongly rooted in them that they couldn't hold back from taking it out on us, so we never have to give it life again? We can stop these things in their tracks before we continue to bring them into the lives of our young ones. Before we spread them via our influence in people's lives. We all touch the world, after all. Whether we want to or not, whether we like it or not, we touch the lives of the people we interact with and our touch spreads through them, to the rest of the world, be it negatively or positively.

We see this in preschool children who mimic others, attempting to soak up all the "how to be a person" from their peers and caregivers and environments. We see this in animal communities when several members learn a new skill and, suddenly, they *all* know the skill. We see this when someone angry makes us angry, when someone smiling makes us smile, and most importantly, when someone plants a seed of change and growth in our lives. This planting of a seed is the kind of lesson that, we can understand later with hindsight, was growing in us for a long time, thanks to the subtle influence of someone who touched our lives way back when. Like a seed, it takes time and growth to thrive and flourish; it takes time before we are blooming in a new way.

These seeds are planted everywhere in our lives. I mean, think about how our parents (and other role models) shaped our lives and personalities from the very beginning. The older I get, the more I hear my mother's voice when I open my mouth to speak to my children. Or my grandmother's laugh. Once in a while, my Aunt Deb's confidence resounds from me. Or my father's stubborn strength and pride. We channel the influences of those who touch our lives. They become part of us. And they radiate from us, touching the lives of everyone around us.

A good example of this is a young girl who's had a rough upbringing. Merely by existing, she's been taught by her life, her own people, and her social status that she doesn't mean much, in this world. Maybe she lives in a home that's fueled by conflict, she has negligent parents who feel like they barely make it by, or maybe she's growing up severely poor. Just one caring teacher can touch the heart and self-esteem of that child forever when she treats her as if she is valued and valuable, as if she is respected and respectable, as if she is worthy and needed. One teacher treating her like an equal human being can show that child what it's like to know that about yourself. It plants a seed of self-worth that grows within the muck of believing she is less than good enough. That memory of care and respect stays with us. It grows with us, eventually blooming when the time and environment are right.

This is one of the main reasons my life feels so deeply meaningful, having worked with young children for so long. Not only are the neural pathways of the brain being developed exceedingly quickly

193

during the first four years of life, but so is the child's foundation for their lifelong sense of self-worth. So *much* of who they are and will be is built in the first few years, through love or through fear and neglect. So, every time I touch a child's life with love, I touch the world with love. Every time I am kind and patient and joyful, this means, and every time I am loving and consistent, and every time I show a child they are trusted and valuable as people, I have planted the seeds of self-love and self-worth. Every time I create a fun, loving, safe space for the children I work with, I've protected them from exposure to one that is not.

I like to keep my intentions with *everyone* this kind, honest, and loving, in the awareness that these things are contagious. Why? Because I want to live in a world that's kind, honest, and loving. I long for a humanity -and a world for my grandchildren and great greatgrandchildren- that is kind, honest, and loving! Isn't it time to weed out anything less than those things? Fear and pain and separation have been suffocating the good in this world for long enough. It's time for our precious children to see a brighter and kinder future! It's time for love to thrive. And the change begins one heart at a time. It begins with you and me.

ABOUT THE AUTHOR

Lindsay Swanberg grew up on the shores of California, and moved to Eugene, Oregon in 2002. Raising two beautiful children, she set up shop as a preschool child care owner and teacher, and has been fulfilling her passion in working with children and families ever since.

Lindsay has her degree with a focus, and extra year of studies, on early childhood education and child development. She also has a two-year diploma in herbalism and holistic health. Lindsay is additionally a Reiki Master Teacher and Nichiren Buddhist. Health and well-being at all ages is a beautiful aspect of life.

She's been writing for Love & Embolden at loveembolden.weebly.com, for years, and is finally getting her thoughts and heart out into book form!

Find all of her books on Amazon.com at
https://www.amazon.com/-/e/B07K1HR9TR.

More Books by the Author

How to Start & Maintain Your Own Successful Child
Care Business

~

A Movement of Courage: Connecting More Deeply
for a Happier Life

~

Amongst the Songbirds: A Collection of Poems

~

Adventure of The Water Walker

~

Return to the Sun

~

The Day Robert Became a Monster

~

Self-Love Activation Journal

*Revised 12/1/2020